ALL
MADE
UP

ALL

THE POWER AND PITFALLS OF BEAUTY CULTURE,

MADE

FROM CLEOPATRA TO KIM KARDASHIAN

UP

RAE NUDSON

Beacon Press
BOSTON

BEACON PRESS
Boston, Massachusetts
www.beacon.org

Beacon Press books
are published under the auspices of
the Unitarian Universalist Association of Congregations.

24 23 22 21   8 7 6 5 4 3 2 1

This book is printed on acid-free paper that meets the uncoated paper
ANSI/NISO specifications for permanence as revised in 1992.

Text design and composition by Kim Arney

Library of Congress Cataloging-in-Publication Data
Name: Nudson, Rae, author.
Title: All made up : the power and pitfalls of beauty culture,
from Cleopatra to Kim Kardashian / Rae Nudson.
Description: Boston : Beacon Press, 2021. | Includes
bibliographical references and index.
Identifiers: LCCN 2021003302 (print) | LCCN 2021003303 (ebook) |
ISBN 9780807059685 (hardcover ; acid-free paper) |
ISBN 9780807059821 (ebook)
Subjects: LCSH: Beauty culture—History. | Cosmetics—Social
aspects—History. | Beauty, Personal—History. | Identity
(Psychology)—History.
Classification: LCC GT2340 .N83 2021 (print) | LCC GT2340 (ebook) |
DDC 646.7/2—dc23
LC record available at https://lccn.loc.gov/2021003302
LC ebook record available at https://lccn.loc.gov/2021003303

For Michael,
who fills my life
with love and laughter

CONTENTS

WHY WE NEED TO TALK ABOUT MAKEUP

There is no way to opt out of the influence makeup has on our lives. There is no way to decide that appearance and the cosmetics used to create it don't matter because the choice about how to present ourselves is never made in a vacuum. Beauty trends change over time, reflecting a culture's shifting tastes and priorities, and that in turn affects what people wear and how they are perceived. Tressie McMillan Cottom writes that beauty isn't what you look like; it's the preferences that reproduce the social order.[1] Appearance matters because as soon as someone steps into view, they send visual signals that could trigger unconscious judgments. People may not be aware of what they are presenting to others, but those signals may affect people's lives in big and small ways every day. No one can skip participating in appearance politics—it matters whether someone believes it does or not, whether someone thinks about it or not, whether someone wants it to or not. No one can stop themselves from being seen.

People face the question of what to wear, and where to wear it, every day. Intuitively, many people know to wear something different to a party with friends than to an office job. This seemingly built-in understanding of socially appropriate self-presentation in ever-shifting contexts likely comes from years of conscious or unconscious data gathering. People see what others are wearing and often try to emulate the generally accepted style. Makeup is a simultaneous reflection of our understanding of the world around us and a presentation of sense of self within that world.

In a video tutorial from Rihanna's makeup company Fenty from December 2019, actor Amandla Stenberg demonstrates a makeup look inspired by New Year's Eve. She says she wants the look to be celebratory and "all about the glitz and the glam."[2] She uses a blend of blue eye shadows to create a cat eye shape that extends beyond her eyelid. The lighter, brighter blues are toward the inside corner of her eye and the darker blues toward the outside. Her dark blue eyeliner comes to a sharp point, extending the length of her eyelids. Her lipstick is a cool, purply brown topped with a clear iridescent lip gloss. Her makeup is colorful and bold, and she sets it with powder so she won't sweat it off while dancing. New Year's Eve can be an excuse to wear glitter and bright colors—parties waiting for midnight may call for glamour that would look out of place in daytime hours.

In a different video for *Vogue* from June 2020, actor Lucy Hale shares her everyday routine for skin care and makeup. In her video, she says that this makeup look is one she'd use for work meetings. She blends a variety of pink eye shadows over her eyelid, and when she applies a shimmery pink cream shadow to her lower lash line, she warns the viewer about going overboard with the product by saying, "This is still day, we don't want to look like we're going to the club."[3] Hale implies that makeup worn for a night out at a club or party is more about excess and bold colors and shapes, while makeup for a daytime work meeting is less colorful, uses less product, and is less obvious.

Hale actually uses eighteen products for her makeup look, while Stenberg uses only twelve. But Hale's colors are more muted—light pinks to Stenberg's bold blues. Hale's eyeliner rims her eyes and doesn't go outside the lash line, while Stenberg's eyeliner extends past her natural eye shape. Hale's makeup look is not quite natural, but its colors and shapes blend with her skin tone and features. But as Hale notes, what could take her look from meeting appropriate to club ready could be just a bit more product than she used in the demonstration. For example, a winged eyeliner may work for the office, but if that wing extends too long, it becomes a cat eye that's not welcome at most office jobs. What differentiates makeup for work versus makeup for a party is the *appearance* of excess, not actual excess. Hale's daytime look uses more products and has more steps than Stenberg's New Year's Eve look, but Stenberg's makeup is bolder. Understanding the difference can be easy in theory but difficult to navigate in actuality. The lines between day makeup and nighttime party makeup are blurry—and not just because they are expertly blended like Stenberg's eye shadow.

Often, when socially acceptable clothing and makeup are required, they cost money and knowledge that the dominant culture hoards. A proper appearance is also often based on upholding whiteness and maleness as the de facto way to be. Appropriate versus inappropriate is a line that can shift at any point depending on who is setting the boundaries—and who is crossing them. Differences in informal dress codes for various events can also be subliminal and hard to elucidate. Generally, attitudes about what makeup looks are acceptable in certain settings reveal more about society's prejudices than about makeup itself or the individuals who choose to wear it. Makeup becomes a litmus test for how people feel about race, gender, sexuality, femininity and masculinity, and more.

Even when many rights and social customs are taken away, makeup remains a touchstone for bodily autonomy, self-worth, and people's and society's priorities. In prison, women often have limited or no access to makeup—but some inmates still find ways to create it from what they do have available. US commissaries in federal facilities in the 2010s may have offered limited products such as lip gloss or concealer, while state and county facilities were likely to offer even fewer options, mostly mascara and eyeliner. So women used things like melted Jolly Rancher candies mixed with body lotion, ground-up colored pencils mixed with baby powder, and coffee mixed with face cream to create hair gel, eye shadow, and foundation, respectively.[4] This creativity in making oneself up in prison isn't limited to a single time or place. In 1977, Linda Maxwell, an inmate of Bedford Hills Correctional Facility for Women in New York, recalled how she used toothpaste mixed with ink on magazine pages to make eye shadow and black shoe polish for mascara.[5] In Milan in 1908, an imprisoned woman made contraband rouge by soaking the red thread of her prison uniform in water and using it to paint blush onto her cheeks.[6] Women in the prison also licked the whitewashed walls of their cells and chewed the lime fragments to create a white paste they used on their faces.

A newspaper article about the incident at the time marveled that these women would be eager to be fashionable even though they never saw any men. "In all other respects most of the prisoners are devoid of every trait which ennobles and beautifies the lives of women," said the story, headlined "Vanity, Too, Laughs At Locksmiths."[7] The writing implied that women only cared about beauty to gain attention from men and that wearing cosmetics in prison was an act of vanity and coquetry. But in prison, wearing makeup wasn't for men's benefit. Instead, these women wanted to look and feel beautiful for themselves and to establish some normalcy and a sense of self-worth. For them, beauty wasn't frivolous or vain; it was survival.

Women are often socialized to protect and encourage their beauty, but in prison the tools to do so are denied. "Society teaches women they have to be beautiful to be worth anything, and then once they're in prison, we mock, demoralize, and punish them for trying to keep to that standard," wrote Marlen Komar for Racked in 2018.[8] Makeup is one of the things prison takes away. That a prison attempts to strip people of their individuality and autonomy by not allowing personal decoration shows how important it is. To go without it is a punishment—self-invention is only for the free.

As these women in prison show, makeup is a tool to create appearance—but it's also a lot of other things. It's a form of control over others and the self, and it's a way to reveal and instill values. Makeup also has a lighter side; it represents creativity, providing community and fun. Many people who use makeup also do it as a form of self-care, using the time they apply cosmetics to pay attention to themselves. In the 1920s, cosmetics companies in the US advertised face masks by emphasizing that while wearing them, women should sit down and rest, wrote historian Kathy Peiss.[9] This created a time when women were able to take a break from housework, their families, or their jobs—a moment where they had no other obligations but themselves. Peiss wrote that one husband, not understanding his wife's interest in face creams, asked her if it was to please men or to make to women jealous. Her response was that she did it to please herself.

Makeup is accessible for many. It comes in different price points, it has many different uses, and it's temporary and can be washed off with soap. Cosmetics can be homemade or store bought. Makeup's flexibility is one of its greatest assets and is partly what makes it so widely used and appealing, both for reinforcing power structures and for trying to survive them. Makeup can be prominent and brightly colored or it can be almost invisible on someone's face. Much like its history, it can be ignored or overlooked even when someone is steeped in cosmetics. The "wrong" makeup can cause funny looks or lead to harassment, while the "right" makeup can be completely unnoticed and unremarked upon.

Media and the wider world often send the message that makeup is necessary for a woman to present a serious or respected front. It can be difficult to constantly see messages from advertisers, media, and regular life that a face without makeup is ugly or incorrect. "What did it mean, I wondered, that I have spent so much of my life attempting to perform well in circumstances where an unaltered female face is aberrant?" wrote Jia Tolentino for the *New Yorker* as she remembered wearing makeup at gymnastics meets as a child and for college interviews as a teenager.[10] Television news anchors even work with image consultants so their appearance doesn't become a "distraction" from the story they are trying to tell—the wrong makeup would be a misstep, but worse would be a woman with a bare face. Going through the process of becoming camera ready can be harrowing—and so is the idea that a person's face can keep them from being hired or being listened to. "I was told I have creepy eyebrows," said one woman anchor.[11] A man was told to lighten his hair because that was the market's preference; another woman was told to lighten her lipstick colors.

As women all over the modern world gained more freedom to work outside the home, they have had to navigate how to enter offices that were previously male-dominated spaces. In certain cultures, makeup became a way to maintain femininity while doing things— like work—that society previously considered unfeminine. Women were conditionally allowed in these spaces—if they maintained the femininity people feared they'd lose by taking on these predominantly male roles. These same women were often relegated to being known as "office girls" and were punished or harassed for daring to take on a new role that transgressed society's idea of what women should do. Wearing the "right" amount of makeup was a way to walk the line between feminine and masculine, home life and work life, being professional and being seen as a flirt.

But there is no "right" version of makeup. Whatever a person wears can be deemed too much or not enough by those in power, with no clear standard. With an extra misplaced swish of a makeup brush, makeup becomes ready for a party instead of the workplace. Either wearing or not wearing makeup often leaves women fighting to be seen for their abilities instead of their appearances. Makeup is both required and stigmatized, and the rules change depending on the race, sexuality, and gender presentation of the person wearing it.

In fact, the best-case scenario for many who wear makeup—like news anchors—is to be unobtrusive and to fit in with the world around them so they can be seen for who they are and not what they are wearing. This makes everyday makeup use sometimes difficult to discuss. Many understand, even unconsciously, that to wear makeup is to gain social standing—and, in the right circumstances, respect. But making oneself up in a way that calls attention to the words being spoken rather than the lips they're coming from can be a challenging balance to strike. Doing so without spending hundreds of dollars or hours in pursuit of ever-changing trends may be nearly impossible. And women are the ones who generally have to bear these struggles and consequences.

In the modern world, makeup is associated almost exclusively with femininity. It represents womanhood and encompasses ideas about civility and respectability, which are bound to gender and race. Because of this association with femininity, makeup is easily dismissed by the dominant culture. Anything typically associated with women's lives—their daily work, their assumed responsibilities and interests, even their taste in food and culture—is often seen as unimportant and silly. Many people of all genders believe that things like makeup and hairstyling are frivolous or only for the vain because they associate caring about appearance with femininity—even though everyone has a body. In reality, men's bodies are set as the norm, seemingly so natural that their appearances don't need to be thought about at all.

Dismissing beauty culture and makeup's history is a form of misogyny and a way of reinforcing stereotypes and systems that keep white men in power. Like other systems of oppression, this form of sexism is pervasive, often invisible, and practiced by people of all genders. Women often deny makeup's importance as they are powdering their faces. Still, something that millions of people do every day *is* important. The multibillion-dollar cosmetics industry is clearly influencing our culture. Even if makeup affected only women—which isn't true—it would be worth looking at closely. In reality, makeup affects everyone, whether they wear it or not.

The tools of masculinity and femininity often overlap, but studying how those tools are used in context reveals the traits a culture values and encourages in different genders. Camouflage paint may seem to have higher stakes than winged eyeliner when it comes to proper application—but that depends on the situation. Camouflage paint may keep a soldier from being spotted by an enemy who would shoot to kill. A woman's life may also be in danger if she doesn't blend in with standards of femininity set by other people.

To ignore makeup's influence is to maintain the hold of the patriarchy, white supremacy, and capitalism. McMillan Cottom writes: "Denying these empirical realities is its own kind of violence, even when our intentions are good."[12] Like the wealthy deeming it impolite to talk about money, not talking about the construct of beauty and the tools used to achieve it only benefits those already in power. Ignoring its importance and its effects are part of the charade of makeup—it hides flaws not only on the skin but also in society. Not talking about the influence of makeup is no longer an option when trying to achieve a just world.

———

Sometimes the stories about makeup told by those in power don't accurately represent how people used it. Makeup myths are everywhere because most people don't care enough to bust them. One I kept running into was the story that white suffragettes wore red lipstick to marches in the US and UK in the early 1900s to defy expectations of what a woman should be. This is repeated in books and on websites so often I thought it was true, but I couldn't find evidence supporting this story in any historical sources or by talking to experts on these women and time periods. However, the modern sensibility of women cutely sticking it to the man makes this story sound good. Symbolism was important—and the suffragettes knew that. That's why they likely *didn't* wear red lipstick: so they could maintain pristine white femininity and respectability while asking for their rights. Individual women may have made different choices, but suffragettes as a group wanted to appeal to the dominant culture's ideas of what women should be to show that their femininity wouldn't be diminished as they gained the vote and gained power in the world. Makeup was not yet acceptable for "respectable" (read: white upper-class) women in society, so red lipstick didn't fit the image they were trying to portray.

What the story about the suffragettes wearing lipstick leaves out is that they protected an acceptable version of white femininity that excluded women of color. A year after the march when women supposedly walked proudly with red lips, Black women were ignored or asked to move to the back in a 1913 march on Washington because they disrupted the feminine ideal white suffragettes were trying to impart. The real history of makeup at these marches tells much more about the struggle to vote and to hold onto power than any made-up story could.

It's sometimes difficult to separate fact from fiction when it comes to makeup because the images makeup creates are so iconic they loom large in people's memories and imaginations. Elizabeth Taylor's glamorous portrayal of Cleopatra in the 1963 movie may be more recognizable than the true story of why actual Egyptians wore makeup (no one knows for sure, but it was likely for medicinal and religious reasons). There are a few explanations why stories about makeup may not be as rigorously researched as other topics. One is that the historical resources may not be there. Another is that because makeup is seen as unimportant, people may not hold its history up to the same accuracy standards as they do other things. The story about the suffragettes is charming. But it may not be true. I tried to put only what I knew to be true in this book, and that in turn illuminated other truths about society.

———

To talk about makeup is to talk about power: who has it, who wants it, and who is trying to keep it. This book is a way of bringing these ever-changing mechanisms into focus. Trying to understand people's use of makeup throughout history and the influence it has had on culture and social structures is a way to reflect on people's humanity. People of all genders wear makeup because they are getting something out of it, and the benefit is worth the time, effort, and money they spend. Learning about why people wear makeup sheds light on how people live and how the world is constructed.

It's a big job, and I'm not an expert. As a journalist—rather than, say, an anthropologist or a makeup artist or a historian—I can help others discover these stories and attempt to unpack the meaning of makeup, but I'll never touch on everything interesting or significant about makeup's influence in society. There are quite a few people and themes that I know are missing from this book—and surely many more that I'm not yet aware of. I am limited in how I think and what I know, but I hope this book inspires others to think critically about the importance of makeup—not just in today's world, but also through the ages.

I'm also not an expert on sexuality, gender, or race, but I will open a discussion about the myriad ways cosmetics and beauty culture intersect with these other aspects of identity. To not discuss them would be inaccurate and misleading. Makeup is where all these issues, and more, collide.

Researching this book has been a privilege. It has been clarifying to dig into this history of how cosmetics shape the world and understand more about why the world functions the way it does. To learn about makeup often means learning about women's lives and how women navigate beauty as a method of survival. But a lot of the daily experience of women's lives throughout history has been lost because it wasn't recorded in media that people in power kept safe. People documenting history often did not see women as worthy of study or of permanence; their diaries or letters were not always kept for posterity. This is also largely true for men of color, gender-nonconforming people, enslaved people, or those living under colonization. I've often been frustrated by a lack of information on how people use makeup in certain time periods and cultures. That doesn't mean they didn't use cosmetics or that appearance didn't matter. It means that those without power weren't included in history's narrative and that their day-to-day experiences weren't seen as important by the dominant culture. If appearance politics are not apparent in a society, it's not because they don't or didn't exist. Sometimes evidence of cosmetics has to be searched for.

I'm afraid I've relied too much on the written word—the people who know best how appearance affects their lives often don't have access to editors or book publishers, and not everyone shares the goal of seeing their thoughts in print. Those thoughts are still worthy of inclusion in conversations about cosmetics. Makeup tips and tricks are often passed from one family member or friend showing another. Makeup use itself is often meant to stay hidden. I tried to listen to people from the communities I wrote about and to consider who was telling what stories and why. I tried to use sources that could substantiate how they knew what they claimed, and I thought critically about where that information came from. Hopefully, paying careful attention to what people put on their faces and why honors the people making those often difficult choices.

———

Studying makeup has laid bare the scaffolding that certain stereotypes were built upon. In many cultures throughout history, women were barred from political and economic power. For example, in eighteenth-century England, women couldn't vote and had limited rights to own property. Middle- and upper-class women were shunted from their fathers' homes to their husbands'. One thing these women could control was their appearance—and their appearance greatly influenced the marriage market, which greatly influenced their lives.[13] But as soon as women changed their appearance—or used cosmetics to enhance that appearance to meet certain beauty standards so wealthy men would find them attractive—men accused them of deceitfulness and vanity. In men's view, cosmetics hid the actual value of a woman because her value was determined by her appearance. Women were vilified for showing agency over their bodies in favor of the men who judged those bodies. Cosmetics in this instance became a tool of ensuring survival when independent wealth wasn't an option. Attraction wasn't necessarily for fun or for love; it was to guarantee a home to live in and food to eat. When appearance determines survival, it doesn't seem stupid to care about it. Taking a careful look at how makeup influences culture and how people navigate makeup to gain status, exercise control over the self, and be safer in the world means deconstructing power structures and understanding that what is frivolous to the dominant culture may be a tool for the less privileged.

———

The functions of makeup and its effect on culture are separated in this book to look at them in isolation—but in the real world that's not possible. Makeup can reinforce white supremacy and gender norms while protecting its wearer from harm in other ways. Makeup can provide community and joy while stoking insecurities. The good and the bad are both true and are often working simultaneously. Part of the point of looking to the past as well as the present in these chapters is to illustrate that none of these issues is new. The makeup industry has changed and so have trends and the meaning of wearing certain cosmetics. But throughout history, makeup has been a way to make oneself beautiful, to gain power, to portray resistance, to blend in, to stand out; makeup is a kind of self-expression that changes with the world around us.

With advances in technology like photography, television, and the internet, documentation of and participation in makeup use changed drastically over recent years. Social media platforms like Instagram and YouTube allow people to participate in beauty communities in ways that they couldn't before. Instead of reading the pages of *Vogue*, people become their own publishers and beauty editors. This means that we're seeing truly individualized self-expression via makeup in ways never seen before.

Images people are posting online of their made-up faces are disrupting beauty standards in creative ways. Teenage boys have found communities online where they can try out different makeup looks, experimenting with ideas about gender in a safe space. After watching *RuPaul's Drag Race* on TV, Elliot Ceretti wanted to try out makeup looks and a drag persona for himself. "Instagram was and still is the only way for me to talk and share this with others like me," Ceretti told *The Guardian* in 2020.[14] Others are using online communities to post purposefully ugly makeup looks that question what beauty means. The ugly makeup revolution has found a community online where people can post and look at makeup that champions the strange and grotesque. One photo showcased pink eye shadow topped with tiny white and clear pearlescent spheres.[15] The eyelashes were spindly white, adding to the ghostly mood. Many makeup looks are created to be posted then washed off before going into the physical world. These and other makeup influencers may experiment with makeup only for digital spaces—the looks are ephemeral and meant to question or celebrate the world instead of function in it. These spaces offer a way to make something new with makeup, a way to stand out and create art rather than fit in to get by. This expansion of beauty and makeup creates a good opportunity to think about makeup further and more critically.

If beauty reproduces the social order, then beauty trends can shift to include or exclude certain groups—and we may be in that transition now. Studying makeup reveals why these preferences are in place, who sets them, and who benefits. There is no way to divorce beauty from cultural norms and power structures; looking closer at the tools of beauty is a step toward dismantling those systems. It's time to take that step.

WORKING IT

A 2011 study—sponsored by Procter & Gamble and carried out by Boston University and the Dana-Farber Cancer Institute—showed that "beauty has a significant positive effect on judgment of competence."[1] Beautiful people are perceived as smarter and more capable, and women are judged more harshly than men when they fall short in attractiveness. This judgment on beauty can affect a woman's income, along with her day-to-day experience of work. In service jobs, such as waitressing, attractiveness can also lead to more tips or more shifts. A bartender named Katie who lived in Arkansas said in a 2020 story for *In These Times* that she was passed over for the most lucrative bartending shifts where she worked because managers wanted "cuter girls" to work instead.[2]

However, grooming can help women reduce the gap in the advantage that comes from being conventionally attractive. A 2006 study looked at the effects of wearing makeup on judgments of health, confidence, earning potential, and professional class for white women in the US and UK. The study, by Buckinghamshire Chilterns University College and a research department of makeup company L'Oréal, showed that participants judged that images of white women wearing makeup were healthier, more confident, had greater earning potential, and were more likely to have a higher-status job than white women without makeup.[3] A 2016 study by sociologists at the

University of Chicago and University of California found that both men and women benefit at work from being attractive—but attractiveness and grooming are particularly important for women. This study found that attractive people can earn about 20 percent more than people who have average attractiveness, and that grooming is a good predictor of earnings, even when controlling for other factors.[4] Grooming and spending time on appearance can be just as important as someone's physical looks, but this is more true for women than for men. For women, makeup can help literally make up the difference in both attractiveness and income.

This bonus derived from being attractive helps women more in the beginning of their careers than later on, said Jaclyn Wong, an author of the grooming study, in a story for CNN Money in 2017: "Once women get into managerial positions, positions of leadership, positions of power, beauty becomes a liability because our stereotypes around beauty are that they're incompatible with capability," Wong said. "So if you're too beautiful, maybe you're not that competent. Maybe you're a 'dumb blonde.' That's a lot more true for women than it is for men."[5]

Many women face the decision over wearing makeup at work, often knowing that using cosmetics makes them appear more capable, but that too much could backfire. But figuring out how to balance their appearance with their workload—and figuring out how much makeup is too much—takes time and money that men don't have to spend. A 2014 study from *TODAY* showed that women in the US spend 6.4 hours per week on their appearance, while men spend 4.5 hours per week.[6] A 2017 study by Groupon found that American women spend an average of $313 a month on their appearance while men spend $244 a month.[7] And Black women in the US face greater pressure at work to look "professional"—a word with complicated racial undertones—than white women; Black consumers spend more proportionally on certain hygiene and beauty products than what white consumers spend.[8]

The grooming study found that for both men and women in the US, grooming helps to signal "gender appropriateness" and that conforming to the dominant culture's ideals of masculinity and femininity is rewarded in the workplace.[9] This study begins to articulate what the idea of looking professional means: A professional appearance reinforces stereotypical gender presentation.

This can hurt everyone, but "professional" appearance in the US can be especially risky to figure out for people who aren't white or cisgender. Richard, a gender fluid femme PhD candidate told HuffPost in 2019 about wearing jeans, a short-sleeve button-up, hoop earrings, and lip gloss to work. They received an email from human resources claiming that hoop earrings and lip gloss were against the dress code, but when Richard looked around the office, they saw many cisgender women wearing hoops and lip gloss. "Through its actions, this organization decided that because I was perceived as a 'man,' I shouldn't be wearing certain things, and it used the language of 'professionalism' to enforce its own biases," Richard said.[10] Lip gloss wasn't the problem; it was that someone who wasn't cisgender was wearing it.

Often people are left to figure out the meaning of dress code violations through humiliating trial and error. "When the big firms came calling for interviews, we were advised to wear foundation, blush, a suitably demure lipstick shade, and suitably demure nails," wrote Priya-Alika Elias for Vox in 2018. However, she noted that no one could agree what demure nails meant. Elias wrote that white women weren't that worried about these rules—one white woman said she didn't plan on wearing makeup at all. Elias was a law student learning about the professional environment of Boston law firms, and she knew that women of color were more likely to be deemed unprofessional if they did the same. "Skipping it wasn't an option, but how much of it should we wear?" Elias wrote. "When I wore makeup—even subtle makeup—I was told it was 'too much.'"[11] Elias said that she received advice to blend in with what older women at firms wore, but as a woman of color, she would stand out among mostly white faces no matter what she did. And when she did stand out, people seized on what she wore as a way to reinforce those differences.

Blending in to professional environments is a costly, difficult situation for many. But to not blend in can be even worse. So people often choose to dress stereotypically femininely or masculinely as a way to avoid other issues in the workplace—like harassment, unwanted attention, losing a job, or not having the opportunity to get hired in the first place. Because appearance is tied to employment, it can be too big of a risk for some individuals to push for a change in professional appearance.

When Yoshiko Shinohara started her temp business in Japan in the 1970s, she didn't look like the CEO—or at least, she didn't look like what men who worked in Japanese offices in the 1970s assumed a CEO would look like. Shinohara had to learn to navigate her professional appearance within the boundaries of her culture while breaking boundaries in other ways. A human resources manager remembered seeing her for the first time: "At that time, walk-in sales visits without an appointment were not yet common. Suddenly, an intellectual-looking and sophisticated woman with a smile came in for sales. She was wearing a deep-red short skirt. Honestly, I was knocked out. Her first impression was rather spectacular."[12]

Although she founded her company, Shinohara left her title off her business card.[13] Most people assumed there was a male president back at the office, and she didn't necessarily correct them. At that time in Japan, most companies were reluctant to do business with a woman based on a sexist cultural belief that women weren't committed to work or were unable to do a good job. If Shinohara went along with people's assumptions that perhaps a male boss was back at her office, it meant an increase in sales. These sales eventually led Shinohara to become Japan's first self-made woman billionaire in 2017, at eighty-two years old. In a Kyodo News photograph from a 2008 press conference, Shinohara's hair is short, around her ears. Blush high on her cheeks toward her temples makes her cheeks appear flushed, and deep dusty-pink lipstick defines her lips. Wearing a black printed jacket, she looks polished, professional—and feminine.[14]

Japanese makeup historically focused on whitish smooth skin, black eyeliner, and red lips, but over the years, makeup colors have expanded. In the 1920s, the style of the modern girl emerged, whose looks portrayed social transformation after World War I and Japan's great earthquake in 1923 greatly influenced the economy. Reminiscent of a flapper in the US—and influenced by their style—a modern girl in Japan would wear thin, drawn-on eyebrows, red lipstick, shorter dresses instead of a traditional kimono, and short hair. The modern girl was a type of independent woman who appreciated modernism and consumerism, and her appearance reflected these beliefs. In the late 1970s and '80s, when Shinohara was working to build her company, beauty trends included thicker, natural eyebrows, natural-looking eye makeup, and vivid lipstick in bright red or rose pink. Foundation or powder colors matched skin tones, instead of being white like previous trends. This makeup came to portray a fresh-faced girl with smooth skin and rosy lips, giving the impression of innocent femininity and youth. Even decades later, Shinohara embodied these trends at business events where she was photographed.

In Japan, the housewife is the dominant cultural signifier of femininity.[15] This has long benefited the Japanese state because a caretaker in the home has saved the government welfare costs, and keeping women in the home makes men's jobs more secure.[16] In the early-to-mid 1900s when women began to leave the home or farm to work in businesses in greater numbers, the jobs they could get often emphasized their womanhood. Female bus conductors or clerks in stores, for example, became known as "girls"—a bus girl or a shop-girl. The "girl" suffix accompanied many women as they gained employment in all types of jobs. Many businesses saw hiring women as a way to attract male customers, and men often saw these women as sexual accessories they had access to while going about their day in what were previously male-dominated spaces. Women who worked in offices were seen the same way: office girls spiced up a place that had previously been just for men. Because of this, women often emphasized their femininity to fit into the image of a working "girl": a sexualized woman meant for men's consumption.

Women who worked in factories instead of offices didn't face the same expectations of displaying femininity at work. Factory work in Japan was female dominated and women often lived in dormitories to work in the factory, only rarely interacting with men, who acted as supervisors. Because these women didn't interact as often with men, working men did not see them as challenging roles that were typically masculine; therefore, they weren't put in a position to emphasize their femininity by using makeup. It's also likely that women working long days in factories didn't have a lot of spare time or money to spend on their appearance.

After World War II, Japan's economy grew quickly because of government guidance and interventions that promoted and protected industries and businesses, and more women started leaving the home to work. But Kumiko Nemoto, author of *Too Few Women at the Top: The Persistence of Inequality in Japan*, writes that the cultural dominance of the housewife extended to the workplace, where women filled the roles of caretaker, helper, and assistant.[17] As the economy grew, women balanced traits Japanese culture associated with masculinity—like working long hours outside the home—with femininity in their styles as they entered public areas that were previously dominated by men.

When women's appearances or actions are viewed as masculine, they aren't celebrated the way men are. They are instead punished for transgressing what women "should" be. Whether a woman should emphasize her culture's idea of masculinity or femininity depends on what it would take for a woman to reject the performance of femininity and what other options are available to her in a particular workplace, Nemoto writes.[18] Women who tried to act like men to succeed in the workplace were often punished—unless they balanced masculinity with femininity. For educated women who got office jobs, that often meant emphasizing their femininity and filling typically feminine roles so they could stay in a place they weren't previously allowed in. Women at work were constantly reminded of a "woman's place"—in other words, that they should act as willing caretakers or "wives" who can "get along with" other women.[19] Traditional gender roles in Japan also emphasize that women, no matter their seniority or skill, should remain subservient to men.[20] If a woman didn't fit a soft image of respectable femininity, like Shinohara's rosy lipstick, she likely would not have gotten a job in these kinds of roles, where women's presence was a prized reward for men.

When Shinohara attempted to pitch her company at sales meetings, she assumed the look of an office girl with makeup to match. This allowed her to more easily move in a space where women were valued for their appearance and subservience, not their accomplishments. Had she not looked like someone men wanted to invite in, or had she promoted her accomplishments as founder and president of her company instead of her appearance, she might not have even made it through the door. Her image was a strategy, a way to blend in with stereotypes so she wouldn't be questioned as she did her work. It was a choice—but her choices were limited by cultural and economic constraints if she wanted to succeed at launching her company. Shinohara's makeup and clothing became a shield of invisibility, amplifying her ambition and her power in a system that tried to limit her.

———

Similarly to Japan, workplace expectations for women in the US changed significantly around World War II. During the depression in the 1930s, jobs were scarce, and women were discouraged from working outside the home so that the available jobs would go to men.[21] That began to change during the war, when men left the workforce to go into the military, shrinking the available workforce at the same time that more workers were needed to manufacture items for the war. The government encouraged white women to join the workforce, filling the jobs men had left behind. "Sure enough, all across the country, the public was bombarded with spirited print and radio ads, magazine articles, and posters with slogans like 'Do the Job He Left Behind' or 'Women in the War—We Can't Win Without Them' depicting noble, pretty but serious, female war workers on the job," wrote Emily Yellin in 2004's *Our Mothers' War: American Women at Home and At the Front During World War II.*[22] These campaigns made the work look glamorous, emphasizing femininity while women were taking jobs that had previously gone to men. However, propaganda campaigns emphasized women's traditional roles even while encouraging them to take up new ones.

In the US, like Japan, when some of these women started working, they were called "girls," which feminized and infantilized them. Clerical workers in Washington, DC, who helped with the paperwork due to the war, were known as "government girls." Before these women were hired, women *were* allowed to work for the patent office to do paperwork and cataloguing—but they had to mail in their work so they would never be in the office. As women filled these wartime jobs and entered workplaces, employers encouraged them to maintain their femininity—in part perhaps to emphasize that after the war, a woman's place would once again be in the home.[23] "One article in a Navy shipyard newsletter counseled women to 'be feminine and ladylike even though you are filling a man's shoes.' At Boeing, charm courses were scheduled for women workers," Yellin wrote.[24]

Rosie the Riveter was not a real woman, but the image of the muscular woman with red lipstick and her hair pulled back off her face represented the women joining the workforce, and it appeared in propaganda and other cultural images, like magazine covers. Norman Rockwell's painting of Rosie the Riveter on the cover of the *Saturday Evening Post* in 1943 depicted a Rosie who wore denim overalls, flat shoes, and goggles on top of her head. She held a sandwich as she took a break from work, with her riveting machine on her lap. Her defined muscles and baggy overalls portrayed a more masculine Rosie than other war propaganda, perhaps as commentary on women taking up men's roles. But this Rosie and other versions wore red lipstick—a reminder of femininity that remained despite changes in clothing, hair, and profession. Women's clothing, shoes, and hair had to change for safety while performing factory work. High heels weren't as practical as flat shoes for standing for hours on shifts while using tools that could fall and injure feet. Long hair and dresses could have gotten caught in machinery. But makeup didn't inhibit workers—a woman factory worker could wear lipstick while on an assembly line without putting her safety at risk, making it a practical marker of femininity to emphasize in propaganda.

Decades earlier, fashion trends dictated that lipstick would have been out of place for a woman who wanted to be seen as respectable. Shifting women's roles and propaganda that emphasized makeup helped push fashion trends toward accepting bold lipstick. Instead of the mark of a harlot, it became the mark of a patriot. To boost morale, the government commissioned Elizabeth Arden to produce a makeup kit for the Marine Corps women's reserve. She created a lipstick, blush, and nail polish set that matched the chevrons on the women's uniforms, and she called the color Montezuma Red.[25] Although the government took control of factories to put them to use for the war effort and the US was under rationing that limited its supply, makeup and powder were still made available to raise morale for the women at home.[26] In Germany, under Hitler, women were discouraged from wearing makeup because his Aryan ideal included a clean, bare face. Some women in the US felt it was their duty to defy Hitler by sporting a red lip, and war propaganda told women it was their duty to keep up their appearances for the morale of the men fighting the war.

These factors set up women in the workplace to feel that part of their job as workers and women was to maintain a stereotypically feminine appearance. Similarly to Japan, appearances in the workforce came to reinforce this femininity as a way to be less threatening to men's roles. War work in the US was seen as a temporary patriotic duty for women—especially white married women—and a way for women to be morally responsible and good citizens.[27] It was not meant to structurally change women's roles in the US or to make women more independent, though for some women who now had access to their own money, that's exactly what it did. Makeup acted as a constant reminder of feminine roles and a reminder that once men came home, women were due back home as well.

———

When the war ended, many women left the workforce to take up their place again in the home. But women kept wearing makeup. As rationing and war shortages ended and more makeup became available, more glamorous styles became popular, in part as a backlash against the perceived masculine role of working. Because women were no longer encouraged to enter the workforce where they had to wear pants and pull back their hair, ultra-feminized styles took hold in the US in the following decade. This glamorous styling affected homemakers and women who remained in the workforce alike, reinforcing stereotypically feminine roles that many women are still trying to get out from under. Glamour also often hides the work being accomplished behind a made-up face, acting as a beautiful distraction from the person under the makeup. Just as glamour is more powerful when the effort behind it is hidden, when women who appear glamorous do work, their work is often dismissed as if it took little or no effort.

Flight attendants in the US in the 1950s were synonymous with looking glamorous—which, in the US at this time, meant thin and white, with straight shiny hair and made-up faces. Flight attendants were required to perform their gender, gently providing service while looking beautiful to make passengers feel cared for and special. But this glamorization had the effect of hiding the work they did behind a beautiful image. Five flight attendant activists filed a complaint in 1977, saying, "The airlines would have us believe that we are too glamorous to be considered workers. And the public considers us too frivolous to be taken seriously."[28] The glamour that flight attendants performed on the job reinforced gender stereotypes of women as natural caregivers, of beautiful people being naturally nice and kind, and of women's work not being real work. This same predicament can be applied to many women in the workforce who have to perform aspects of stereotypical womanhood, like waitresses, assistants, or nurses.

Airlines generally hired only young single women, and they could force women to retire by preventing them from being scheduled for any flights if they got married or grew older than an age set by the airline, often thirty-two. One flight attendant remembered undergoing a physical pelvic exam as part of the hiring process to make sure she wasn't pregnant or didn't already have children.[29] Their guidelines to maintain a workforce of young, single, beautiful women were unreasonable and discriminatory, focused on sexualization and beauty.

When they were hired, flight attendants went through a makeover, cutting their hair and applying makeup in a certain way that was standardized across the airline—for example, using approved beauty products and having collar-length hair. Requiring certain makeup was a way of reinforcing the image of glamour that airlines were selling. A flight attendant for Pan Am remembered wearing blue eye shadow to match her uniform.[30] Supervisors regularly checked employees for their weight, uniforms, and other appearance metrics, and they even told flight attendants they needed to check makeup more often during a shift if it was not up to their corporate standard.[31]

The makeover required by airlines could be traumatic for the people undergoing them. One flight attendant with Pennsylvania Central recalled coming back from an all-day beauty overhaul when she and her colleagues burst into tears at the sight of the made-over women all looking like "clones."[32] And indeed a brochure with information about becoming a Pan Am flight attendant from 1967 showed an illustration of a blonde woman with chin-length hair, thin arched eyebrows, eyes rimmed in black, and red lipstick. A photograph on the next page shows a woman with brown hair, but everything else is the same: chin-length hair, smooth red lips, pristine arched brows, and eyes that stand out with black liner and thick lashes.[33]

Airlines enforced appearance standards based on white bodies, such as white skin, straight hair, and a thin body shape. By requiring that flight attendants be attractive with good manners and other subjective skills, airlines set up barriers for those who were not upper or middle class, Christian, and white. "The airline industry had never bothered to specify 'whites only' in stewardess employment, but it did not have to," wrote historian Kathleen Barry in her book *Femininity in Flight: A History of Flight Attendants*.[34] Rather, their hiring practices kept many Black women out of the workforce because white managers did not see them as attractive and white society judged their behavior more harshly than that of fellow white people. For example, in the 1960s and early '70s, airlines didn't allow flight attendants to have Afro hairstyles.[35] These practices were born from racist and sexist ideas that white Eurocentric beauty standards were what customers wanted to see in service workers for expensive services like airlines. They also functioned as an advertisement to the types of customers— white, upper class—that airlines wanted to attract.

The Civil Rights Act of 1964 threatened to upend the way airlines did business when it outlawed discrimination based on race, religion, national origin, and gender. But the law included a clause that said employers were allowed to treat employees differently based on those categories if it was deemed necessary for normal business operations. So airlines said that they needed female flight attendants for a variety of reasons—for example by saying that women were better at performing services, that men wouldn't feel comfortable asking another man to do things like get him a drink, and that people who got airsick would prefer comfort from a woman. Flight attendants were seen as a kind of wife or mother in the air, one that customers could depend on as if she were a hostess at a party. Airlines made the argument that gender was essential to the job, which made it even more difficult to disrupt the gendered appearances they required. And white women fit white male airline executives' image of an upper-class hostess.

Organizations like the Urban League, the National Association for the Advancement of Colored People (NAACP), and the New York State antidiscrimination authorities fought to get a few Black women working as flight attendants in the late 1950s and early '60s. But white women had long benefited from the glamour of being a flight attendant, and airlines and white workers became concerned that allowing Black women into their ranks would somehow denigrate their reputation and the glamour of the job.[36] Even when Black women wore the makeup and hairstyles dictated by their jobs, white folks still claimed that they weren't displaying the correct or ideal version of glamour that white femininity required—because they weren't white.

While glamour often disguised the hard work of flight attendants, it offered other advantages. Glamour provided social capital that flight attendants benefitted from. Flight attendants went to parties with celebrities, and they had access to travel and invitations to exclusive restaurants. Flight attendants represented the American ideal of womanhood at the time, and they received the benefits of being young and beautiful along with the prestige of being associated with the exclusivity of air travel. But holding onto that glamour upheld whiteness as a beauty ideal, and glamour didn't come with workers' rights or fair compensation. Instead, it masked work as fun, pretty, and frivolous and valued the image of the airline over the well-being of its workers.

———

Using makeup to break expectations of gender roles at work can come at a cost, and people of all genders need to decide if it's worth it to them. A flight attendant would likely have been fired, or never hired in the first place, if she didn't follow company guidelines around makeup. Sally Ride, the first American woman to go to space when she flew on the Challenger mission in 1983, decided not to wear makeup on this different kind of flight. Ride had a unique position as she navigated the country's response to a public, professional woman in a dangerous and prestigious job. She remembered receiving questions from the press that had nothing to do with spaceflight and everything to do with sexist expectations of women. "Everybody wanted to know about what kind of makeup I was taking up. They didn't care about how well-prepared I was to operate the arm or deploy communications satellites," she said in an interview with feminist political activist Gloria Steinem soon after her mission.[37]

The entire NASA program was based on men's bodies. When the women in Ride's class of astronauts were preparing to go into space for the first time, NASA made some changes to accommodate them. When the NASA engineers asked if the women's toiletries kits should include makeup, Ride declined to include any in her personal kit. "The engineers at NASA, in their infinite wisdom, decided that women astronauts would want makeup," Ride said. "So they came to me, figuring that I could give them advice. It was about the last thing in the world that I wanted to be spending my time in training on."[38] Ride felt that makeup wasn't a necessary part of being an astronaut, and she felt like it was a waste of effort to spend time on makeup when she had bigger things to do—like safely go to space. She was insulted by the constant questions and assumptions that focused on her womanhood over her status as an astronaut, and it was important to her to de-emphasize makeup and emphasize her professionalism in other ways.

But astronaut Rhea Seddon said she did want to bring some makeup items with her. "If there would be pictures taken of me from space, I didn't want to fade into the background," she wrote on her personal blog years later.[39] Seddon noted that she wasn't the only woman astronaut to use it. Those who opted to use the NASA kits of eyeliner, mascara, eye shadow, blush, lip gloss, and makeup remover may have understood that images of the astronauts would be transmitted or printed in US or global media and that expectations for women's appearances didn't go away even when women left the planet. The first women in the US to train for spaceflight faced immense pressure from the media and may have felt their own pressure to be good representatives for NASA, which in part depended on public perception to get funding. Reasons to wear or not wear makeup all had consequences, and each astronaut had to decide which to bear—something the male astronauts, who were automatically assumed to be professional without makeup, didn't have to consider.

When Hillary Rodham Clinton started her career, she didn't fit into the dominant culture's idea of what a woman should be. She kept her maiden name after she got married, and she didn't wear overly feminine clothing or much makeup.[40] That changed when her husband, Bill Clinton, ran for governor against Frank White in 1982. To help him in his campaign, Hillary Clinton changed her appearance, promoting a more feminized, domesticated woman, and attempted to become a version of herself that the people of Arkansas would be more comfortable with. She had learned that disrupting the image of idealized womanhood wasn't worth it for her at that time, so she leaned into a more feminine appearance to avoid certain conflicts. Clinton kept those lessons with her as she ventured on to her own career in politics. But when she was the presidential candidate herself, she had to balance her femininity with the image of a person who was competent and capable of doing a job that had only ever been performed by men—just like Sally Ride. But unlike Ride, Clinton turned to makeup.

In 2008, in the first Democratic debate CNN broadcast in high definition, Clinton got her makeup done by Kriss Blevens, a makeup artist in New Hampshire who has worked with politicians to prepare them for TV appearances. At this debate, Blevens used a blend of three lip colors on Clinton instead of putting her in her typical nude color. This deep pink, an almost-but-not-quite-red, "had tabloid writers, beauty experts, and people watching at home wondering whether Clinton had surgery or just a really good night of sleep," wrote Claire Carusillo for Racked in 2016.[41] This lipstick became known as "the lipstick," and it changed the conversation around Clinton's appearance once again. People were complimenting her, instead of questioning her femininity or her devotion to her job or the people she served. The lipstick didn't solve Clinton's public perception problem—she would always face detractors, and women who run for office are still judged more harshly than their male counterparts. But this small change may have made her public life a bit easier, and it made people a bit more focused on what she had to say instead of how womanly she was—or wasn't—when she said it.

In a 2014 study, psychologists found that ambiguity about a candidate's gender—even for a fraction of a second—could particularly hurt women candidates in the US. The study said that votes for men were influenced by competency and attractiveness, whereas results for women were influenced by any ambiguity about their gender, in addition to competency and attractiveness.[42] This means that women tend to do better in elections, especially in conservative areas, if they appear more feminine, the study said. This reinforces stereotypical gendered appearance as a positive for someone in a campaign, making running for office a much trickier prospect for transgender or gender-nonconforming people who don't fit into stereotypical images of men and women. Gender conformity—or rather, the appearance of gender conformity—becomes something that can help or hurt a candidate in a split second. Deciding whether to fit into or deviate from masculine or feminine imagery at workplaces can be fraught, and one can risk unemployment and harassment. That the workplace reinforces stereotypical gendered appearances doesn't leave room for anyone who doesn't fit those stereotypes to safely do work, and politics are an extension of that struggle.

For women of color, the unspoken rules around appearance in the workplace are different than those for white women, and so are the risks when those rules are broken. Alexandria Ocasio-Cortez became the youngest woman to serve in US Congress in 2018 when she won the election to represent New York's 14th District, which includes parts of the Bronx and Queens. When she was sworn into office, Ocasio-Cortez wore red lipstick and hoop earrings. "Lip+hoops were inspired by Sonia Sotomayor, who was advised to wear neutral-colored nail polish to her confirmation hearings to avoid scrutiny. She kept her red. Next time someone tells Bronx girls to take off their hoops, they can just say they're dressing like a Congress-woman," Ocasio-Cortez wrote on Twitter.[43]

Sotomayor became the first Latina judge on the Supreme Court when she was confirmed in 2009. Sotomayor actually did keep her nails neutral during her confirmation hearings because President Barack Obama's staff told her she should. Obama's staff was repeating the same advice given to Elias: Wear suitably demure nail polish. But *Latina* magazine reported that "on the day of the White House reception celebrating her appointment, Sotomayor asked the president to look at her freshly manicured nails, holding up her hands to show off her favorite fire engine–red hue."[44] She then also pulled back her hair to display her red and black semi-hoop earrings.

Ocasio-Cortez's and Sotomayor's style choices were notable because they ran counter to the political dress code of muted hues and not overly made-up feminine appearances. But they were also notable because in some Latinx cultures, red *is* a professional color. Pushback against bright nail polish or lipstick in a professional setting in the US may have racial implications: Because Latinx women wear it, white folks call it unprofessional. Ocasio-Cortez and Sotomayor both have parents from Puerto Rico, and hoop earrings and red lipstick and nail polish are symbols of beauty in the Puerto Rican community. "For some, red lips are a reminder of the Latinx stereotypes placed on us by a society that oversexualizes our community.

For others, red lipstick is a symbol of power and reclaiming their culture," wrote Marilyn La Jeunesse in *Teen Vogue* in 2018.[45]

When Ocasio-Cortez and Sotomayor highlighted red lips and nails and hoop earrings, they chose to celebrate their culture while celebrating professional milestones. For Latinx people who were made fun of for their hoop earrings and red lipstick and who didn't assimilate to white beauty standards, Ocasio-Cortez and Sotomayor showed that Latinx women could still wear those styles and be celebrated in a professional setting. "To me, my hoops were an heirloom, until I learned I'd have to set them aside to be taken seriously in certain circles," wrote Frances Solá-Santiago for *Glamour* in 2019.[46] "So when Representative Alexandria Ocasio-Cortez, the Bronx-born Puerto Rican Democrat from New York, was sworn into Congress wearing a white pantsuit, a red lip, and big gold hoops, it wasn't just a good look—it was a radical act." Wearing bright makeup in professional settings where more muted makeup is standard is a risk. It's especially a risk for women of color, who face greater pressure to appear professional and who face racism as well as sexism in the workplace.

———

In certain Latin American societies, makeup bolder than the muted tones seen as professional in the US may be popular in some workplaces. A well-groomed appearance is emphasized in places like Brazil, Ecuador, and Venezuela, and effort put into grooming is celebrated and respected rather than hidden like in the US. A common saying in Ecuador and other Spanish-speaking areas in Latin America is "there are no ugly women, just poorly groomed ones."[47] Cosmetics like red lipstick are a clear indication of the artificiality of beauty and become a marker of the effort put into going beyond a natural appearance. This is reinforced throughout the region with the popularity of beauty contests as a way to bring prestige and wealth to those who participate. In these contests and elsewhere in the postcolonialized region, makeup is used to reinforce whiteness and class.

In addition to reinforcing gender and race, makeup at work is important because it can indicate class. Makeup can be a visual marker of the consumption that is tied to wealth, and women may use it to appear to belong to a higher class whether their economic circumstances actually support that or not. For poor women who have limited resources, their body is something that is under their control, and they can use their appearance to fit into the image of a higher-class, professional woman to get work.[48]

For women in Ecuador who work for the direct sales makeup company Yanbal, a well-groomed appearance is emphasized as part of the company culture. Women are encouraged to use the Yanbal cosmetics that they sell, and many women believe that they should appear as if they are making money to be trusted as successful salespeople. A Yanbal salesperson may be expected to remove hair from their bodies and faces, use deodorant and Yanbal perfume, and care for their nails. They are encouraged to tie long hair back from their faces, and if a salesperson dyes their hair, they should maintain their dye so their roots won't show. Salespeople are expected to wear makeup, such as lipstick, eye shadow, and mascara. Using these cosmetics implies that the salesperson has a certain level of income that allows for these purchases.

Yanbal salespeople are also seen as belonging to a higher class than women who sell at markets, and their appearance reinforces this distinction. "Many market women in Ecuador wear variations of indigenous dress, which is associated with low class status and a stigmatized ethnicity," wrote Erynn Masi de Casanova in 2011's *Making Up the Difference: Women, Beauty, and Direct Selling in Ecuador.*[49] Race, as well as class, is tied to appearance, and an appearance that is considered "professional" separates higher-class workers from those who labor or work in markets.

Nail polish is a cosmetic that is a particular class differentiator. Middle- and upper-class women in certain areas in Ecuador are "almost never seen with fingernails and toenails in disarray or unpolished."[50] A professional appearance indicates that nails should be covered with fresh polish or should be clean with no polish. Chipped nail polish or unkempt nails are clear violations of professional attire—and visual indications of physical labor, instead of higher-class, less laborious work. Lower-class women will paint their own nails, and higher-class women will pay to receive manicures and pedicures to fit into this standard.

Direct sales companies like Yanbal and Avon had a large influence on culture in certain Latin American countries. By using door-to-door sales, these companies could reach working-class women, Black women, and women who lived rural areas, democratizing access to makeup and giving these women a chance to use it to meet professional-appearance standards. The communal nature of door-to-door sales also provided discussions about how to use makeup, sharing application tips and trends that previously may have been siloed in upper classes. These companies may also have offered payment in installments, making cosmetics more affordable by breaking up the price into smaller chunks paid over time. This allowed women who didn't have access to a professional appearance to acquire the cosmetics to create one—while keeping them tied through debt to the company they worked for.

When workers are in vulnerable positions, the question of whether to wear makeup takes on greater importance. In Hong Kong, migrant domestic workers can face strict rules about how they act in their employer's home. These rules may include when to bathe, how to greet the employer's family, and what clothing and makeup they are allowed to wear during work. In the 1990s in Hong Kong, the majority of domestic workers were foreign women. In *Maid to Order in Hong Kong: Stories of Migrant Workers*, Nicole Constable wrote that in 1995, there were more than 150,000 foreign domestic workers in Hong

Kong, and more than 130,000 were from the Philippines.[51] Instead of leaving the home to enter public spaces for work, these women left their own homes to enter the homes of their employers. Their workplaces were not dominated by men in public areas; rather, they included the private sphere of domestic work and family. As such, their professional appearance was dictated by different standards than forms of employment that took place outside the home. Professional appearance for these domestic workers was set up to maintain class differences that kept the worker clearly in a lower class. Because both the workers and the employers were generally women, feminized products like makeup could become a particular battleground.

Filipina domestic workers would often work with agencies in the Philippines and in Hong Kong to be trained and then placed in homes for work. Applicants were evaluated on a number of invasive measurements such as weight and HIV status, and they could be required to take a pregnancy test. Applicants were also encouraged to lose weight, trim fingernails, cut their hair short, and remove makeup.[52] The makeup and clothing applicants were encouraged to wear acted as class markers. Requiring domestic workers to wear their hair short with no makeup went against feminine appearance standards in Hong Kong of wearing makeup and having long hair. Deviating from cultural standards indicated that the worker appeared subservient and as part of a lower class than the employer. Where a woman office worker may have needed to emphasize her femininity to fit into a male-dominated space, a domestic worker ended up desexualized and plain to be allowed to work in a home, often under the control of another woman.

Some women used makeup as a way to carve out some control over their own lives under the strict rules of their employer. One worker that Constable spoke with liked to dress differently than the ascribed dress code for domestic workers of jeans and a T-shirt. She wore dresses, blouses, skirts—and some makeup. But she experienced complaints from employers who said, "She's only a maid; she doesn't have to use makeup!"[53] A lack of makeup was so clearly associated with the status of domestic worker that wearing it caused complaints that a woman was attempting to appear as if she belonged to a higher class.

Across many cultures and time periods, makeup becomes a visual cue that can reveal status, wealth, and power. Often women have to use makeup as a way to gain control over their lives, be allowed in certain spaces, and just be able to do their jobs. A professional appearance can help an employee get and keep work, but that appearance is often predicated on reinforcing race, class, and gender in ways that maintain those social divisions. Women are often obligated to fit into these appearance standards so they can work and make money—a ransom disguised as a choice in patriarchal societies that too often keep women from economic independence. To navigate these appearance standards, women spend more time and money than men do to receive the same benefits at work. Often, these standards affect women of color, transgender people, and gender-nonconforming people more than white cisgender folks. What looks like playfulness to some on the outside can mean the difference between a raise or dismissal to employees, tying economic security to knowing to wear the correct shade of lipstick.

HEY, SEXY

It's impossible to know someone's inner thoughts and emotions based on their appearance—and generally that's for the best. But on occasion, appearance can also telegraph meaning and hidden desire. People may make themselves up to signal romantic interest, attract the attention of a potential mate, and expose emotions without having to say anything out loud. Chemistry between people is an invisible feeling, but makeup can illustrate an attempt to make it visible.

Smudged lipstick and blush can mimic the flush of sex; glitter and highlighter can catch the eye of someone from across the room. A theory among some psychology researchers claims that people's "attraction to sparkle" comes from the innate need to find water.[1] Light dances across liquid the way it may scatter across someone's ruby red lips, quenching a different kind of thirst. These visual signals can attract the glance of a partner, but more than that, they can communicate a desire to be looked at.

Wearing makeup itself can be a sensual experience. Fingers pat and smooth down lipstick, and brushes sweep gently over eyelids. This pleasure can be for oneself, but putting together a makeup look can also show other people that an effort was made to appear before them. Ideas for "date night" makeup supply endless tutorials and tips, indicating an impulse to know what makeup to wear and how best to attract a romantic interest. Knowing how to enhance or minimize certain body parts can make someone feel more beautiful and confident.

Depending on the context, the same makeup can come to mean different things for the person wearing it and the people looking at them. Lipstick on a white married woman can become a symbol of domesticity and femininity, while lipstick on a white married man could be viewed as a marker of homosexuality. Eyeliner on a white woman and a woman of color are not read the same way because they have a different history and face different prejudices. White women's sexuality is protected in the US, for example, while the sexuality of women of color is often villainized. The excessive cat eyeliner on Elizabeth Taylor in the 1960s started a craze, with fans clamoring to see more of her and copy her makeup to capture the sexuality she exuded. But the heavy eyeliner worn by Mexican American girls in the 1940s—after Mexican Repatriation, the mass deportation of Mexicans and Mexican Americans between 1929 and 1936—added to white people's prejudices and was seen by many whites as evidence of delinquency and prostitution.[2]

In popular culture, female sex symbols are created in part from the makeup they wear. In the US, Clara Bow's pouty bee-stung lips, Theda Bara's smoky eye shadow, and Marilyn Monroe's red lips and big eyes made more dramatic by false lashes all epitomized sexiness in their time and pushed the previous boundaries of makeup. In Life's 1958 Christmas issue, Richard Avedon photographed Monroe made up to look like five previous Hollywood sex symbols. The images illustrated how makeup for sex symbols can shift over decades—and that makeup was key to inhabiting their on-screen presence. Monroe dressed up as Bara, Bow, Marlene Dietrich, Lillian Russell, and Jean Harlow, recreating an iconic image of each of the movie stars.

In her tribute to Bara—a silent film star and Hollywood's first sex symbol—Monroe sported a dark wig and a bra top and flowy skirt similar to what Bara wore when she starred in 1917's *Cleopatra*. Monroe's brown eyes peer out from underneath thick black eyeliner making a circle around her eyes and extending past the outer corners. Her bold thin, dark eyebrows angle upward, and her lips are painted red. This makeup mirrors the look that Bara became known for, called the vamp, or vampire. The contrast of dark eyes and lips against a pale face made expressions clear in black-and-white silent films, and the heavy eye makeup transgressed the Victorian beauty ideals of a face with no makeup. *Life* said that Bara represented "all the women who came bursting from their stays in World War I with predatory eyes and heavy make-up into new freedom."[3] Bara's heavily shadowed and lined eyes broke a boundary and created a new extreme. The same could be said for her sexuality, which was open and visible for moviegoers. Bara's eye makeup was the precursor to the modern smoky eye—a sultry smudged style of eye shadow that tempts onlookers to meet the eye. A smoky eye could be seen on a date in the 2000s, an echo of the lasting influence of Bara's sex appeal.

Monroe herself became a famous sex symbol because of her body, her personality—and the cosmetics she used. Monroe's eyebrows are softer than Bara's, though still thin, and the hairs feather naturally in a soft brown. Her thin black eyeliner lines the lashes of her top lid. Her eyelashes are made longer on the outside corner of her eye by false eyelashes, opening up her wide doe eyes to seem even larger. Monroe had a mole on her cheek above her lips, which she sometimes highlighted by coloring it with makeup to make it stand out more. Her painted mouth is a bold, shiny red, and her peroxide blonde hair tops off the look. Her signature makeup is so iconic that it's recognizable in costumes and drag performances, with her lipstick, hair, and beauty mark portraying Monroe's sex appeal no matter who is wearing it.

To achieve her voluptuous lip look, Monroe likely used a combination of several lip colors. The darkest red lined the outside of the lips and shaded the corners of the lips. Lighter reds filled in the lips, with the lightest red in the center of the bottom lip. On top of the middle of the bottom lip—the fullest part of the lips—went a dab of highlighter to attract light and make the lip glisten. These colors were blended, giving the lips a seamless look that had dimension, making them seem fuller than if they were all covered in the same shade. The same technique is used in contouring the cheekbones or nose: darker colors go on the edges and an iridescent material goes on the high part of the cheeks or the center of the nose, where the light hits.

All of the "fabled enchantresses" that *Life* included in its photographs used cosmetics to emphasize their eyes and lips, two points of connection for communicating with other people. Their makeup, meant for the movie screen, was exaggerated and party ready. The heavy makeup these stars wore may not have been appropriate in daytime settings, but it could have been a style people felt comfortable wearing for an evening date. Its excess added to the stars' glamour, and their eyes and lips became features that viewers wanted to copy with cosmetics of their own in an attempt to procure some of the actors' sexuality and star power for themselves.

The cosmetic industry has long associated makeup with sexuality as a way to sell its goods around the world, leading sexuality and makeup to become intertwined in media and further reinforcing their connection. This was particularly true in the US after World War II. Advertisements for makeup during the war focused on maintaining beauty as a show of patriotism and strength; cosmetics were a duty that had little to do with individual self-expression. After the war, advertisements began to shift to depict the erotic. One groundbreaking advertisement from Revlon in 1952 emphasized sexuality to the mainstream US culture. The ad showed the image of white model Dorian Leigh in a silver sequined evening gown that clung to her body. She wore the red lipstick and nail polish that Revlon named Fire and Ice. The ad asked, "Are *you* made for 'fire and ice'?" and a questionnaire followed, asking women questions like "Have you ever danced with your shoes off?" and "Do you close your eyes when you're kissed?" If a woman answered yes to at least eight of the fifteen questions, she was deemed ready to wear the "lush-and-passionate scarlet" of Fire and Ice lipstick and matching nail polish.

This ad placed women's sexuality in their own hands, making them the protagonists of the ad and of their appearance. "As Revlon executives explained, the aim of the ad was to show 'There's a little bit of bad in every good woman,' and lipstick would help you unleash it," wrote Madeleine Marsh in *Compacts and Cosmetics: Beauty from Victorian Times to the Present Day*.[4] As other companies followed suit, advertising in the beauty industry became increasingly focused on tying sexuality and makeup together. This, along with movie screens, caused an influx of images of women's sexuality and the cosmetics to create it.

———

Although sexuality was present in advertising and in movies, women didn't necessarily have an easy time owning their sexuality in public life. When women use makeup trends to attract or stay beautiful for a husband, it's generally seen as respectable and acceptable. When women use these makeup trends to attract multiple men, or women, or to please oneself, or if a man wears makeup, the dominant culture in the US often judges them to be "too sexual." The makeup may not change, but depending on the context, it becomes the marker that onlookers use to accept or denounce someone's sexuality.

In the US during World War II, women entering the workforce were encouraged to maintain their femininity by wearing lipstick. But when women wore lipstick in a different context, the meaning changed. For women who appeared to transgress their societal role of devoted wife and instead showed sexual independence, makeup stopped being patriotic and instead became a symbol of their sexualization.

During the war, women were encouraged to support their country by working in factories, maintaining their looks, and socializing with servicemen. But this socialization often led to blurred lines between acceptable behavior and behavior that was deemed "too sexual." The government, along with individual men, encouraged women to provide for men's sexual needs, going so far as some people encouraging teenage girls to have sex with soldiers before they went overseas as a way to contribute to the war effort.[5] The US Public Health Service physician Otis Anderson created the term *patriotutes*—combining patriot and prostitute—to describe women who entertained troops to maintain morale. This term, and people's attitudes about unmarried independent women socializing with men, often stigmatized the women who were fulfilling a call for support—for example, by going to dances at military clubs. These women, also called "victory girls," may have worn lipstick to show their patriotism, especially if they felt they were supporting the war effort by beautifying themselves and socializing with soldiers. But for others looking at them, lipstick may have indicated the overt sexuality of young women wantonly spending time with men.[6]

During World War II, the government also campaigned against the spread of venereal disease—and women alone were seen as vectors spreading disease. This made women's sexuality seem inherently dangerous. Because of this and already existing judgments of women's sexuality, increasing numbers of women were arrested on "morals charges."[7] Lower-class women in certain professions, like waitresses or laundresses, and especially women of color were often targeted as being hypersexual, but generally it was difficult to articulate what made a woman suspicious. In theory, any woman could be suspected of being a patriotute—"respectability" wouldn't provide protection in a culture that saw any woman in public as a moral and medical threat.[8]

Experimenting with makeup in the 1940s often indicated a girl or woman who was embracing modernity—for example, by going to work to support her family while her husband was away. But when the state identified female sexuality as a threat to the war effort, these same women were targeted for abuse. Women found to be transgressing sexual norms—by waiting on men in public, walking with a man in public, or just existing, alone, in public—were punished by being jailed, quarantined, hospitalized, forced to undergo medical testing, turned over to social workers, and surveilled.[9] The same lipstick someone wore to go to work and maintain femininity could be evidence of sexual activity outside the workplace, leading to harm to the person wearing it. Unable to keep up with shifting expectations, many women suffered severe consequences—even death—for others' interpretations of the intent behind their appearance.

———

Whether makeup actually indicates a desire for sex may change depending on the culture and time period, just like makeup trends themselves. In ancient Greece, as in modern times for many women, ideal femininity was constructed through clothing, makeup, and hairstyling. The ideal skin tone for women was white, often with the aid of white lead cosmetics. This white makeup could also be used on the neck and arms to give the appearance of a white skin tone all over the body. Most women also likely wore rouge to give the cheeks a rosy complexion. White skin indicated wealth for white women because they did not need to go outside to perform labor. It also may have signified a woman who conformed to social standards and was therefore "submissive, modest, and chaste."[10] White skin and red cheeks were therefore cosmetics of chaste, respectable women. Sex workers and other "disreputable" women may have used different cosmetics to communicate sexuality instead of chastity.

Cosmetics were gendered items and generally were used by women at this time in ancient Greece. It's likely that most women in the classical and Hellenistic periods wore cosmetics, but class and status as a "proper" woman were defined by the amount and type of cosmetics women wore. An aristocratic woman would have likely limited her cosmetic use to conform with the appearance of her class. A woman who wanted to emphasize her sexuality would likely be identified by her excess cosmetics use and her use of black eye makeup.

In Greek culture, gaze was connected to sexuality, and a woman would have lowered her gaze around men to demonstrate her modesty. Eye makeup, such as lamp black or kohl to define eyelids or eyebrows, would have drawn attention to the eyes—a source of impropriety for women. Drawing attention to the eye with makeup also demonstrated agency. A woman in charge of her own gaze and where she chose to look was a powerful signifier that she was also in control of her body. Because of this, eye makeup was inherently seen as sexual, and those who wore it became associated with sex.

Eye makeup was part of a construction of an image of sexuality, similar to how Bara used heavy eye makeup to create an image of sexuality in the US in a different time period. But in the modern US, women have both greater sexual freedom and more freedom to express themselves with makeup. However, there are still social customs around what makeup is appropriate to wear at certain events. Generally, heavier, bolder makeup is more associated with evening social activities, like parties or a date. That this makeup is socially acceptable for evening activities may give people the impression that it's tied to romance and sexuality, which these activities were sometimes meant to encourage.

When people wear what's perceived as nighttime makeup in the daytime, it can be a violation of social customs. In certain societies, violating dress codes is associated with violating moral codes, and makeup can become a visual indicator of illicit things that happen when no one can see. One 2017 study showed that both men and women in the US perceive women wearing makeup as more open to casual sex outside of a relationship than women who don't wear makeup.[11] This may be a reflection of the custom that makeup is appropriate on dates where women may be performing beauty and creating a sexual persona. This study also found that men were inaccurately more likely to assume that attractive women were more open to casual sex. The study said this could be in part because of wishful thinking on the part of men who were attracted to women: if they found a woman attractive, she'd be more open to a sexual relationship. Makeup is part of what creates a vision of femininity and beauty for many women, and if men believe that's attractive, their own desire for a sexual relationship may color their perception of what makeup means when others wear it.

This same study found that makeup is not an accurate indication of actual sexual habits. Women in the study self-reported their willingness to have sex, and it didn't line up with what the men assumed when looking at their made-up faces. There is not one trend that may indicate sexuality, and sexuality may not be decipherable in makeup at all. Not everyone wears makeup on dates or wears makeup to feel attractive. In *Elle* in 2018, twenty-five-year-old Kate said she likes a more natural look on dates to remind herself that there is no need to try to be better or different than she normally is and that her natural self doesn't use a lot of makeup.[12]

Sexuality is part of the construction of beauty and femininity that many people create when they wear makeup. But since it's not the only reason people wear a certain kind of makeup or makeup at all, making assumptions about people's intent can be difficult. Instead of one trend depicting sexuality, makeup that indicates sexuality may have more to do with cultural norms and customs and when those customs are broken.

Feminine sexuality is often defined by a calculated construction of glamour through makeup, styling, and body modification through piercings, jewelry, and sometimes cosmetic surgery. Beauty ideals are often on display in popular cultural symbols like the stars on TV and in the movies—and in some cases, these cultural icons end up creating new beauty ideals that are reflected back in the population again. This cycle is particularly evident in Venezuela, where beauty pageants have shaped the broader population's concept of beauty to the point where the country became known as a "producer of global beauty queens."[13] Beauty queens have in turn brought money and positive publicity to Venezuela, in addition to creating an image of beauty and sexuality that influences the general population.

"Transformista" has different meanings in different countries in Latin America, but in Venezuela, it describes a woman assigned male at birth who works to transform her body to fit into feminine ideals of womanhood in Venezuela by doing things like plucking eyebrows, wearing makeup, taking hormones, getting breast implants, and wearing women's clothing.[14] The word also has associations with sex work because many transformistas may have difficulty getting jobs outside of sex work. Not all trans women are transformistas—and outward appearance does not define gender—but transformistas participate in Venezuela's notions of what it means to be glamorous, and they leverage that glamour to carve out space for themselves in Venezuelan culture. Transformistas participate in the kind of made-up glamour mainstream culture prizes, but instead of creating an image to be judged at a pageant, they create an image to be in control of their sexuality, gender, and lives. Both transformistas and beauty contestants take care to perform the kind of femininity that is highlighted in Venezuelan beauty pageants, and both use their sexuality to create a presence—the beauty contestant on the stage, and the transformistas on the street.

Part of the construction of beauty and sexuality for both beauty contestants and transformistas often involves body modification. Scholar Marcia Ochoa found that some of the beauty contestants used makeup to cover up bruises on their legs from a weight reduction massage and injections.[15] Cosmetic surgery or other procedures are common in Venezuela, especially for beauty pageant contestants. It's unlikely that a contestant would need to hide that she had undergone a cosmetic procedure; rather, the makeup is used to cover up the coloring of the bruising and to reinforce the image of perfect, unblemished skin, which helps create the image of a young sexual woman whose pristine naked skin could be on display.

Transformistas may undergo many of the same cosmetic procedures as cisgender women beauty contestants would. It's common for transformistas to get breast implants, for example. But transformistas also often need to function outside of medical systems that may have rules about gendered surgeries. This environment may lead transformistas to operate largely on their own outside of the medical community when it comes to body modification—for example, by injecting substances like olive oil under the skin to enhance breast shape. Some transformistas get procedures done by a doctor, some women perform a self-administered feminizing regimen outside of the medical system, and some women undergo a combination inside and outside the official medical system, depending on the access they have and rules they choose or are able to follow.

The appearance of gender and sexuality becomes something transformistas have control over. Transformistas emphasize the performance of femininity in public settings, taking the production of the beauty pageant off the stage and into public spaces. The makeup transformistas use reflects the construction of a feminine public persona that highlights control, spectacle, and sexuality. Some of the transformistas Ochoa spoke with who worked as sex workers wore silver lipstick with black lip liner.[16] This color emphasizes the theatricality of their appearance. Beauty pageant contestants tend to wear somewhat traditional lipstick colors of red, brown, and pink. The silver on the transformistas highlights the active construction of their beauty; there's no need to pretend it's natural when beauty is clearly created by the person wielding it. The women pose on the street, sometimes bearing bare breasts and torsos, showing off the bodies and personas they've created.

In addition to prejudices sex workers face, transphobia and sexism lead transformistas to have to figure out ways to operate outside of the dominant culture. To find a niche, they use their bodies, appearing ultra-feminine to create a presence in public spaces instead of being ignored or passed over. Transformistas actively participate in creating a glamorous image to receive the societal benefits of being beautiful and sexy. Cosmetic procedures and bright lipstick create a feminine appearance based on the culture of Venezuela's beauty pageants, but it is modified to fit within the transformistas' community. Their silver lipstick helps create the look they need, signaling that their sexuality is on display and that they created it and are in control of it.

———

Whereas for women, makeup can be part of a performance of femininity that emphasizes sexuality, for men who wear makeup, certain cultures can see it as a symbol of sexual deviance from straight masculine norms. For modern cultures in which makeup has become associated with women and femininity, men who wear makeup are perceived as defying masculinity and can be targeted for criticism and worse.

In London in the 1920s and '30s, powder puffs and other cosmetics were used in court as evidence of male homosexuality. In one case, a twenty-three-year-old man named Thomas was imprisoned for three months on charges of homosexuality—for "importuning male persons for an immoral purpose."[17] The officers who arrested him presented a powder puff, powder, and a small mirror they'd found among his possessions at the time of his arrest as evidence of his "deviant character." In doing so, the police contributed to the narrative that men possessing or using makeup was effeminate, and that effeminate men must necessarily also possess "illicit sexual desires."[18] Carrying makeup symbolically marked Thomas as gay just as much as his actual actions did.

Thomas's mother claimed that the makeup was hers, but her claims didn't stop Thomas from being condemned because of his association with makeup. Cosmetics were used as evidence in dozens of similar cases in London between the two world wars. Other men were found to be carrying face powder, rouge, or eye shadows, all of which were used in court as evidence to prove homosexuality. Whereas evidence in court for other crimes was connected to the actual act of committing a crime, makeup in these instances was instead used to prove an association with the "type" of person who would carry cosmetics—a person who defied straight sexual norms.

There is no fixed meaning of rouge or lipstick, and even in the courtroom where these items were presented as evidence, the meaning was not always agreed upon. The accused offered other explanations for carrying makeup, such as for its medicinal or hygienic purposes or that it helped men meet standards of appearance for their jobs, such as an actor or waiter. Cold cream, for example, could be used after shaving to relieve skin irritation, and antiseptic powder was advertised to men to soothe skin. Waiters powdered their faces sometimes to look clean and improve their appearance while serving high-end customers, and actors used greasepaint and powder for roles.

However, gay men often *did* wear makeup as a way to construct their own personas in a culture that attempted to define it for them. Gay men used makeup as a way to distinguish themselves, create their own identity, and find others who accepted their sexuality. Wearing makeup also allowed gay men to be visible in public and to create a presence in a culture that attempted to keep their sexuality hidden or underground.

In the 1920s and '30s, makeup was easier to obtain and carry around than in years past because of advances in production and technology, making it more accessible for people to use in ways they could define for themselves. Makeup made visible what was invisible, both for LGBTQ people and for those who wished to use makeup to condemn them. Makeup became a way for the dominant culture to target and oppress queerness and to police men's sexuality, as well as for gay men to define their own culture and communities.

———

The makeup of subcultures can help members find each other, similar to the way makeup can help attract a romantic partner. During the 1940s, at the same time white women wore lipstick to their factory jobs to maintain their femininity at work and victory girls were sexualized because of that same red lipstick in a different context, the pachuca style became prominent in certain Mexican American

communities. The makeup of a pachuca didn't attempt to assimilate into white culture or try to appear white. Pachucas "seemed to
parody the understated updos and subtle makeup of everyday women
and Hollywood starlets," wrote historian Elizabeth Escobedo.[19] Instead of assimilating or hiding their heritage, pachucas created a
"distinctly Mexican American subculture."[20] For some women, the
pachuca look of short skirts or pants and dark lipstick that pushed
the boundaries of propriety was a way to indicate rebellion, including
sexual openness.

Pachucos were Mexican American men who help popularize
zoot suits and were rumored to be associated with gangs, criminal
activity, and rebellion from the "conformity and austerity" of the
war years.[21] Zoot suits were draped outfits with high-waisted pants
pegged at the ankle and long fingertip coats. In addition to the racist reactions to Mexican Americans and Black men wearing these
suits, their excess fabric at a time when the US government tried to
redirect fabric to use for the war led them to be deemed by some as
unpatriotic.[22] The female counterpoint to these men were pachucas,
who became known as independent, sexualized, rebellious Mexican American women who wore modified styles based on the zoot
suit, including fingertip-length coats, tight V-neck sweaters, skirts
that were above the knee, and sometimes high-waisted pants. These
women also wore their hair in a high pompadour, had thin plucked
eyebrows, and sported dark red lipstick instead of a bright patriotic
red. Their makeup use was heavier than makeup styles in the dominant white culture, mirroring the excess of the zoot suits.

Mexican American women during World War II were experi-
encing a similar shift in public life as white women. Many women
were entering public spaces to work and expand their social roles,
but daughters of Mexican immigrant parents may have also faced
strict rules like chaperoned dating that came from Mexican culture
and the Catholic Church. When these women entered the workforce—and were encouraged to mingle with men going off to war—
they may have used the zoot suit styles to experiment with their new

social roles and stake a claim on public life.[23] Many Mexican Americans experienced a shift in their home lives as well, where women's roles relaxed and expanded outside of the virginity-to-domesticity path that lay ahead of them before the war. The pachuca style was a form of freedom for some women and included a sexuality that differed from the restraint of their parents' generations. One young pachuca girl continually ran away from home with her friends, in part to dance with pachuco boys.[24] Juvenile case files suggest that many pachucas engaged in sexual activity, often in steady relationships with Mexican American men.[25] The heaviness and boldness of their makeup in the daytime may have contributed to an image that these women were willing to break social norms, including sexual ones.

Not everyone who wore the style viewed herself as a pachuca—some women embraced the sexual liberation of a pachuca while others condemned it, and some women just liked the style. But the perception of a sexual, rebellious women followed their appearance, no matter who the person was underneath the lipstick. Older immigrant generations strongly condemned the supposedly sexually lax pachucas and their betrayal of "proper female behavior."[26] Certain Spanish-language newspapers "likened the young women to prostitutes, asserting that their male companions served as pimps," and the English-language newspaper the *Los Angeles Evening Herald and Express* wrote an exposé on "the alleged promiscuity and delinquency of barrio women."[27] In 1942, a Mexican man was found murdered near a water pit known as the Sleepy Lagoon. In connection with the case, "police rounded up hundreds of second-generation youths of Mexican descent."[28] Law enforcement investigated ten women, most of whom had Spanish last names. The presence of young women and girls of color between thirteen and twenty-one years old in the spectacle surrounding the murder shocked the larger population.

A photo of three of the women arrested during the Sleepy Lagoon investigation clearly illustrated that the women wore the same style. Dora Barrios, Frances Silva, and Lorena Encinas each wore their hair in a pompadour, lifted high off their foreheads with the rest of their hair flowing down their backs. Their dark eyebrows were plucked to a sharp arch, and two of the women had white makeup outlining their eyebrows and lips to make the dark color of their groomed brows and painted lips stand out even more. The publicizing of the Sleepy Lagoon case amplified the degenerate reputation of pachuca women and reinforced the public's view that the women were involved in gangs, tying the image and style of the women with criminality and sexualization.

The fear of overtly sexual Mexican American women was stoked by racist fears of miscegenation, or any sexual relationship between two people of different races. Although laws prohibited interracial marriage in most states at the time and social taboo further discouraged any potential romances, the general perception of the sexuality of women of color seems to have triggered white women in particular, who felt their prominent place in the culture as emblems of idealized beauty was threatened. The reputation of the pachuca became so pervasive that Mexican American women often needed to grapple with the image of the pachuca whether they wore the style or not.

The modern "spicy Latina" stereotype echoes and mirrors that of the pachuca woman, using lipstick as a way to continue to condemn and police the sexuality of Latinx women. The "spicy Latina" stereotype in the US depicts the image of a woman with light-brown skin, large hips and breasts with a small waist, long straight hair, and red lipstick. The stereotype also imagines that this woman is fiery, sexual, and passionate. This image is repeatedly portrayed in US movies and television, narrowing the image of Latinx women in public. A 2016 study from USC Annenberg School for Communication and Journalism found that in movies and TV shows from major US studios, only 5.8 percent of speaking roles went to Hispanic or Latinx characters but that Latinx women were more likely than white, Black, and Asian women to be sexualized through their clothing in those roles.[29]

These media portrayals influence the way the dominant culture sees Latinx women in real life. Marilyn La Jeunesse wrote in *Teen*

Vogue in 2018 that, as a teenager, she heard students at her school "calling other Mexican American students slurs based on their red lip–big hoops combination," and she wasn't brave enough to wear red lipstick herself until her freshman year in college.[30] In La Jeunesse's article "21 Latinx People Get Real About What Red Lipstick Means to Them," Sandy Gonzalez said her conservative Mexican parents told her growing up that red lipstick was promiscuous. She didn't start wearing red lipstick every day until she was twenty-six. When other people see a Latina woman with red lips, they often use that presentation as a reason to continue oppressing Latinx people.

Makeup becomes a proxy for society's beliefs about sexuality, a visual signal that stands in for what's hidden. That includes making homophobia and racism visible. White people often use makeup to reinforce racist stereotypes that sexualize people of color. The same makeup that defines respectability for white women can become evidence of "too much" sexuality when a woman of color wears it. White people then use the idea that women of color are overly sexual to continue to dismiss and oppress them.

In the US, white enslavers sexualized Black women and girls by using their bodies as a way to increase their wealth—by forcing enslaved Black women to have children who were also enslaved and claiming that it was due to their increased sexuality compared with white women. As Black people gained legal rights after slavery ended, fears of miscegenation were prominent in white US society, and media in the white dominant culture promoted imagery that reinforced racist beauty standards and the sexualization of Black women. Black women in the US continue to grapple with sexist and racist stereotypes, often unable to wear makeup and be in public without battling anti-Black images and attitudes. Red lipstick in particular became a marker of this sexualization. But lipstick can also be a way for women to take control of their appearance and define their own sexuality.

Red lipstick on Black women represents a convergence of these issues of racism, sexualization, and sexual agency. Society in the US has sent a message to Black women that thick lips are an undesirable feature. In minstrel shows after the Civil War, white actors exaggerated the size of their lips when wearing blackface makeup, and thick lips on Black women have often been sexualized or mocked. Black women, especially those who have dark skin, have been told repeatedly in society that they shouldn't wear bright red lipstick, or that their lips are too big to be considered beautiful by white mainstream standards.[31]

For some Black women, whether to wear makeup that draws attention to their lips can be a difficult decision. Teryn Payne wrote in *Glamour* in 2018 that for her, after learning about minstrel shows in school, "it's not all that shocking that to this day there are still certain lip colors I won't wear, like light pink or red, because they draw too much attention to my mouth."[32] When MAC Cosmetics posted an image of Ugandan model Aamito Lagum wearing dark purple lipstick on the company's Instagram in 2016, the post received a flurry of racist comments about the size and shape of her lips.[33] The purple is a deeper color than a bright red and, in theory, attracts less light and less attention. But the racist remarks reveal the real issue: it's not the color of the lipstick; it's that a Black woman took pride in her lips and colored them at all.

When Rihanna's makeup company Fenty launched in 2017, it sold a lipstick called Stunna Lip Paint in a bright, bold red. The company calls the red Uncensored and says it's a "perfect universal red."[34] Choosing to lead her products with a bright red lip color—one that is meant to work on every skin tone—is bold for many reasons. From the beginning, Rihanna chose for her company to highlight her lips—a feature that has been a sensitive topic for many Black women. Rihanna chose to amplify physical features of Black women instead of downplaying them or assimilating to white beauty standards.

Rihanna also uses herself in some Fenty ads. With that, and with social media and red carpet appearances, Rihanna shows how Fenty makeup can be worn by Black women like herself in a variety of situations. She's using her celebrity power to make cosmetics on Black women a part of the media landscape. And when Rihanna wears makeup, it's glamorous and fun—she shows mainstream culture that a Black woman can be someone to aspire to.

In a video posted to YouTube in 2018, Rihanna shares a makeup tutorial for a look that has blue eye shadow and bright red lips. With her red-nailed manicured hands, Rihanna paints her upper lip with Stunna Lip Paint. She uses the wand to trace her cupid's bow first, saying that she wants the height of her lips to be even. She holds a compact mirror in her hands and focuses her eyes as she fills in her upper lip, then her bottom. "There's always that little bit of imagination that your lips are kissable—that's my favorite thing about Stunna Lip Paint," she says after she talks about how the lipstick will keep a slight sheen on the lips throughout the day.[35] In putting the lipstick on herself and teaching others how to do so, Rihanna is taking her makeup and her sexuality quite literally into her own hands. Instead of worrying about society's judgment, which often deems Black women's lips too big or too sexy, Rihanna controls how she views herself and how she creates that image.

Makeup becomes a lightning rod for impressions of sexuality, because wearing it is a visual, concrete action that can portray something hidden, like attraction. Wearing makeup to be seen in public can be regulated through social rules and etiquette, and breaking or tweaking those rules can communicate ideas about community, identity, and sexuality. Generally, the more makeup someone wears, the more sexual they are assumed to be by others, as if daring to take up visual space leads to sexual freedom. While makeup can be a way to express community and individuality in a way that includes sexuality, it does not define sexuality—only people speaking for themselves can do that.

EXPANDING GENDER

The idea that makeup is a feminine product is so entrenched in culture that, to some, a made-up face encapsulates what it means to be a woman—but the world hasn't always been this way. Historically, makeup has been used by all genders for a variety of reasons, some of which didn't have to do with making gendered distinctions at all. Makeup trends can reflect the values of a culture, along with ideas of beauty, respect, and who gets to be seen. When makeup is limited to one gender, it limits the lived experience of all genders, creating distinctions and boundaries where none existed before. The path of makeup becoming feminized in the modern world reflects a world made smaller by placing restrictions on who can define gender and who has gender imposed upon them.

In certain historical cultures, makeup wasn't gendered at all. Ancient Egyptians are well known for using eye makeup, and cosmetic containers have been found in tombs for men and women. Drawings and sculptures illustrate eye makeup in a thick eyeliner surrounding the eye and extending past the outer corner, sometimes in a thick line extending toward the temple and coming to a sharp point, akin to a modern cat eye shape. Eye makeup at this time was likely green or black. In addition to beautifying, this eye makeup was likely medicinal. It protected the skin from sunburn, and certain materials, like lead and copper ore, had antibacterial properties that could prevent infection—though too much of those elements could be toxic. Egyptians also used oils to protect the skin from the sun and to keep skin moisturized, and perfumes and scented oils were used by men and women. Makeup in this culture could be for religious ceremonies and everyday health care, in addition to creating a pleasing appearance—but it likely wasn't a part of defining gender.[1]

Historically in certain Indigenous American cultures, body paint and tattoos were also worn for reasons that didn't indicate gender—for ceremonies or to note accomplishments, for example. In some cases, social roles would be indicated by body paint or other ornamentation no matter the gender of the person participating; gender as Western societies understand it may not have existed at all. (That said, there were many Indigenous American tribes with different cultures and beliefs, and for some, ornamentation was a binary gender marker.)

A contemporary term to describe Indigenous Americans whose gender exists outside of colonial definitions is *Two-Spirit*.[2] Two-Spirit is a term that may also encompass LGBTQ people, depending on the context, and it can also indicate gender that falls outside of the gender binary. Two-Spirit people were not necessarily bending the social norms in their communities; in some tribes they were a regular part of those norms. In some Indigenous cultures, like the Chumash, Two-Spirit people would have historically filled certain roles *because* of their gender, becoming a needed and respected part of the community. However, just as there is not one definition of a generalized Indigenous American person, there is not one uniform definition or experience of Two-Spirit people.

For the Chumash and other California tribes, Two-Spirit people had a significant role in society as people who were responsible for death, burial, and mourning rituals—undertakers of the community. The journey to the afterlife made up a series of experiences by both male and female supernatural entities, so third-gender people, known as *'aqi* in Ventureño Chumash, were the only people who could perform the ceremonies because they lived in male and female spaces, and they were held in high regard.[3] Post-menopausal women may have also been considered 'aqi, indicating shifting gender lines and boundaries that could change over time.

It may have been difficult to tell 'aqi from Chumash women because they were dressed and made up similarly. For California tribes, body paint may have been associated with religious ceremonies, but it also could be a social activity that all genders participated in. The Chumash in particular may have used white, black, red, and other colors of paint, sometimes in lines or dots across the face or body, among other designs.[4]

Two-Spirit people have existed throughout history, but historical documentation of Two-Spirit people has been tinged and erased by colonization. In addition, Indigenous people may not have documented their cultures in the same way Eurocentric societies did, and many histories were passed down orally instead of in written form. Understanding more about Two-Spirit people often means reimagining and reconstructing history from biased first-person sources and archives that often came from colonizers of Indigenous Americans.

When Western ideas of gender and gender presentation clashed with Indigenous cultures during colonization, colonizers may have used makeup to define and enforce gender on Indigenous people in harmful ways. This gendered violence illustrates the harm that can come from associating makeup with only one gender and from enforcing gendered distinctions at all.

In 1775, a Spanish soldier wrote in a memoir about the Chumash people. The soldier wrote that he had evidence that Indigenous American men had been observed in the dress, clothing, and character of women, and that he knew of a few in each village. He called them *joyas*, a Spanish word for Indigenous men dressed up as women, and he believed that Indigenous people held them in great esteem—but he viewed them as deviant. "The abominable vice will be eliminated to the extent that the Catholic faith and all the other virtues are firmly implanted there, for the glory of God and the benefit of those poor ignorants," he wrote.[5]

He believed that he saw men in women's clothing, but he may not have understood what he was looking at. The Spanish soldier may have been looking at Two-Spirit people—but there is no way to know. Spanish colonizers viewed Indigenous Americans as mentally, physically, and spiritually inferior. They did not understand the Indigenous cultures they came into contact with and didn't attempt to learn about them. Instead, they opted to enforce their Eurocentric views and beliefs onto the Indigenous people they encountered, often violently. This included ideas about gender.

In 1513, explorer Vasco Núñez de Balboa came across about forty Indigenous people that, in his belief, appeared to be men in women's apparel. He ordered his dogs to murder them. This violence was one example of colonizers causing harm to Indigenous people because of their gender. Third-gender people were not only killed by disease or starvation caused by colonization but also were actively sought out and killed by colonizers.[6]

It's impossible to know for sure what Balboa saw when he looked at this group of people. But punishing Indigenous people who violated colonizers' ideas of gender norms was common. Consequences of being seen as a joya included flogging with a leather whip typically as thick as a fist, time in the stocks, and being placed in a device that restricted movement but allowed the person to work, wrote Deborah A. Miranda, who is an enrolled member of the Ohlone-Costanoan Esselen Nation of California.[7] Other punishments included forced repetition of prayers, verbal harassment, and ridicule in front of the joya's community. Colonizers would also force the joya to dress and participate in the gender grouping that the colonizer deemed appropriate—forcibly misgendering joyas and placing them in the wrong group, Miranda wrote. Forcing joyas to wear clothes that didn't fit their roles and gender was a way to control their gender presentation and force them to assimilate to colonizers' culture. When colonizers narrowed the meaning of gender presentation, they were exterminating a culture and a way of life. Instead of expanding what gender could mean and allowing space for survival of all genders, colonizers made the definition of acceptable gender presentation narrower, endangering the lives and cultures of Indigenous people.

Two-Spirit people who did not fit into colonizers' ideas of the gender binary were often the first targets of colonizer violence. When European colonizers misinterpreted gender presentation or enforced their own gender roles onto Indigenous people in what is now called the United States of America, it became a form of gendered control. Part of this violence may have come from white colonizers misreading body paint and facial tattoos because they used Eurocentric stereotypes and assumptions about cosmetics and applied the gender binary where it may not have applied.

Cherokee warriors historically wore facial tattoos to keep a record of people killed, scalps taken, or other military records. Drawings of Cherokee people show facial tattoos that are thin lines—sometimes horizontal repeating lines across the forehead or diagonal lines across the face. Throat and sternum tattoos were particularly prominent for Cherokee people. Other Southeastern Indian tribes may have used similar markings, but the reasons and placements for the tattoos varied by tribe.[8] Women could be warriors in Cherokee culture and sported similar tattoos—they were not limited to men. But when white colonizers saw these women, they likely applied their own understanding of strict gender roles that didn't include women as warriors.

In addition, colonizers applied their own understanding of gender roles to sexualize Cherokee women, often using their own association with makeup as a feminized practice as a way to colonize Indigenous women's bodies. Colonist William Bartram's descriptions of Cherokee people eroticized women and girls and framed their descriptions as being attractive and sexually available to white men. This applied a binary, patriarchal lens to gender that could only see women as sexual objects in the service of men, applying gendered and racist expectations.

Bartram described seeing a group of Cherokee girls collecting strawberries and said they were "staining their lips and cheeks with the rich fruit. The sylvan scene of primitive innocence was enchanting, and perhaps too enticing for hearty young men long to continue idle spectators."[9] This description mirrors the use of lip color and blush in Anglo-American societies, and women in the late 1700s who wore colorful makeup like blush were generally overly sexualized. This reading of the girls' strawberry eating reinforced the image that Cherokee women and girls were sexually available. The description of makeup where none existed implied the threat of sexual violence and gendered control.

When people use makeup to help create or enforce gender roles, they are defining ways people are allowed to live, which can either create great freedom or instill harm. Using makeup to indicate or define gender was not universal, and historically makeup has been used by all genders. By associating makeup with one gender, all genders may become restricted in gender presentation and acceptable behavior.

In the modern world, makeup has taken on an association with femininity and womanhood—a stark contrast with certain historical cultures. For thousands of years, makeup went in and out of style for all genders depending on the culture and time period. The idea that exclusively women should wear makeup took hold as a standard and spread around the world beginning in the modern cosmetics industry around the late 1800s and early 1900s. In Anglo-American societies, makeup had typically been more associated with femininity than masculinity, but in the eighteenth century in England, both genders wore makeup like powder and rouge in the wealthy aristocracy. Colonists in the US mimicked that styling as well with things like powdered wigs. During the American Revolution, beauty ideals began to shift, with patriotic men rejecting symbols of the monarchy, including excessive decoration.[10] Men in leadership positions didn't need to display their authority, and both men's and women's virtue was thought of as inherent, without the need for artificial aids. Men and women were using their appearances to indicate their values—the brighter future they aimed to create rejected the monarchy both in practice and in appearance.

However, women were still judged by their beauty—outward appearance was meant to indicate the goodness within. And if a woman's worth was dependent on her looks, it's likely that some women used cosmetics to subtly achieve that "naturally virtuous" glow. Makeup trends encouraged women to wear cosmetics that quietly enhanced natural features instead of heavy makeup. Use of any cosmetics was hidden as much as possible, so that a woman could claim that her beauty was all natural—and her value all the greater as a result. Men were less inclined to spend time on covert cosmetics, since their livelihoods never depended on their attractiveness in the same way.

In the nineteenth century, gender roles in Anglo-American society became further defined, with women in control of the domestic sphere and men the public sphere. Wealthy Victorian men shunned decoration, while women turned increasingly to ornamentation in their clothing but not on their faces.

Perfume started to be gendered too. Historically, men and women both used perfume and used the same scents. But as bathing more often became more popular in Europe in the nineteenth century, men used soap, eau de cologne, and scented oils instead of perfume. Women started using floral perfumes, in contrast with the less sweet scents men seemed to favor, further entrenching gender roles.[11]

As industrialization took hold and modern factories and businesses came into being, society shifted again. Social mobility became more possible, and women started gaining power as consumers. Expensive perfumes became a marker of luxury and an aspirational product. Department stores became a place where white women could shop, giving them a public space they were welcome in, instead of being confined to the home. Makeup and perfume were sold at department stores, though for the most part colorful cosmetics were still an indication of an overly sexualized lower-class woman, or someone violating gender norms, according to the dominant culture. Salons, pushed in part by cosmetic titans Helena Rubinstein and Elizabeth Arden, also became places where women could socialize in public with other women—and where they could get their hair or makeup done or exercise. Taking care of one's appearance gave upper-class women an acceptable reason to be in public that wouldn't hurt their reputation. In fact, it would likely help their social status to be well groomed and beautiful. Appearance became tied to women's new social roles; makeup and beauty became a ticket to the outside world and a new way to live. For women who couldn't easily shop in department stores—Black women or women who lived in rural areas, for example—door-to-door sales took hold as well.

Advertising in the modern beauty industry also emphasized femininity and tried to appeal to a person's womanhood. The creator of moisturizing face cream Nivea Creme, Oscar Troplowitz, emphasized emotions in his advertising for the product, creating a "Nivea woman" who was elegant and vulnerable and who suggested to women that using face cream could make them more feminine.[12] Ads took advantage of women's growing buying power, and advertising companies knew women were a group that could be targeted to increase sales. It was easy to disprove advertising claims if they were based on whether a product worked to clear skin or remove spots or wrinkles—and even if a product did work, its impact may have been small or taken time. It was a lot harder to prove a product did or didn't make someone more feminine or womanly.

While society was shifting in these small and great ways, advances in technology with electricity and photography meant that people could have a clearer image of what they actually looked like. Appearance and images became more important because they were more accessible and could spread in magazines, posters, and movies like never before.

With this push into mainstream consciousness, cosmetics became a respectable way to achieve daily beauty, instead of existing mainly in the realm of the socially ostracized. This was part of imagining a new future for women that changed what the dominant culture viewed as acceptable. Colonization around the world helped spread this message, along with Eurocentric beauty ideals that emphasized cosmetic use for women. In a period of around one hundred years in Europe and the US, makeup started becoming associated with women and desirable beauty. And over one hundred years later, the connection between women and makeup remains.

———

To use makeup in the twenty-first century is to engage in some way with femininity because of how gendered the modern makeup industry became. Part of interrogating whether a person feels comfortable using makeup is to ask how it relates to gender and gender expression and what gender presentation may mean to the wearer. This conversation is always mutating, depending on the culture and time, and how an individual grows and changes. Makeup is a powerful tool for instigating that conversation by providing a means of creative self-invention.

Meredith Talusan wrote that after she transitioned in 2001, she was obsessed with her femininity. She said that she reveled in using makeup and clothing to express herself in ways she hadn't felt comfortable doing before she came out as trans. But eventually, she "grew weary of the awful feeling that my beauty was always on the verge of collapse, that a mere rub of the eyes or bunching of the cloth would ruin the effect."[13] During her transition, she said she "perceived the reality of womanhood only from outside" and that she had idealized femininity to feel like she belonged among women.

Eventually, she began to see that there is no one model of what a woman should be, and that any presentation of womanhood can be true to the specific woman she is at a certain point in time, even if she didn't wear makeup at all. "Making those judgments for myself is at the core of why I transitioned to be a woman in the first place: to express my gender how I want to, regardless of society's expectations," she wrote.[14] Once she grew assured that her womanhood came from within, she knew that no matter how she appeared on the outside, she would always be a woman to herself. For Talusan, not wearing makeup was the truest form of expression for her gender—at least for who she was for a certain period of time. Choosing to wear makeup—or not—can be a way to define gender for oneself and defy gender expectations.

———

In certain parts of the world, increased use of makeup has helped to recreate the cultural meaning of masculinity. In Asia-Pacific, men's use of makeup has increased in recent years, according to 2019 data from Coresight Research. Sales of men's grooming products is expected to increase 7 percent by 2022, and men in China, Japan, and South Korea are leading the charge.[15] Korean beauty especially often prizes clear, moist, buoyant skin that indicates youthful perfection. Many men who use makeup are generally sticking to products like BB cream and eyebrow pencils, gel, or powder. BB cream can even out skin tone and can hide imperfections and pores. Eyebrow pencils can add definition to an ultra-groomed look.[16] These products can create a natural look—though perhaps unnaturally enhanced—that helps men project an image of control and attention to detail, attributes that often pay off in a business setting. Many men think of these products as skin care—as natural a part of their daily routine as shaving or washing their face.

This shift in masculine ideals and appearance in East Asian countries like Japan, China, and South Korea has been occurring over decades—just like in every culture, gender and gender expression is a living, changing creation. With the expansion of the economy and a shift to modernity in the decades after World War II, masculinity began to take the shape of a well-groomed, sometimes aggressive professional—like the archetypes of a "salaryman" for Japan or a "white collar beautiful man" for China.[17] These images of masculinity depicted a professional man who looked after his appearance—but who wouldn't have worn makeup. These versions of masculinity depended on consumption and could be achieved only with money and the time to spend on taking care of appearance. This ideal depicted the image of someone who worked hard in an office job and could afford to wear things like Armani suits and Rolex watches.[18] This image also reflected Western ideas of modernity. This was in part based on increased globalization and an increase in business travel all over the world.

Men depicted these new ideas of what was masculine in the late twentieth century by wearing well-cut suits, expensive watches, and prioritizing grooming, rather than overt decoration, for skin, hair, and the body. Cosmetics may have included face wash and moisturizer but likely wouldn't have included visible or colorful eye shadow or lipstick. Increased attention to grooming would have been one way to illustrate wealth and status.

Although these men may not have been focusing on a physical representation of strength or violent aggression, they still practiced a form of masculinity based on intense competitiveness that placed men at the top of the system, wrote scholar of masculinity Kam Louie.[19] Although typical gender presentation for men may have changed over decades, there is a through line of competitiveness and being on top of a societal structure.

With a rise in internet use and culture in the 1990s, as well as an economic slowdown in countries like Japan, ideals of masculinity in popular culture began to shift again. In the early 2000s, instead of prioritizing the image of an office worker committed to working hard to get ahead in corporate life, some men began to show a lack of interest in making money or prioritizing sexual relationships. In Japan, these men were called "herbivore men," a term created by writer Maki Fukasawa. Fukasawa said that unlike their Baby

Boomer parents, these men were not as assertive or goal-oriented, in part because they grew up during an economic recession instead of an economic boom.[20] There were fewer jobs available, and dressing professionally likely didn't help much in achieving the lifestyle their parents prized, so their appearance and goals changed. As part of their style, some herbivore men wore makeup that emphasized a softer version of their fathers' masculinity. Paying even more attention to their looks and using makeup to express themselves may have been a way to increase confidence when previous markers of success were no longer available to a new generation.[21]

In addition to these factors, pop culture was changing, and new ideas of masculinity came from anime, television, and pop music. One example of an herbivore man that had cross-country appeal was Tsuyoshi Kusanagi, a member of Japanese pop musical group SMAP, which was also popular in Korea and throughout Asia. The five-member pop group formed in 1988, and in the decades since has helped recreate both the pop landscape and masculine ideals in pop culture. The members also appeared on variety shows and worked as actors, and Kusanagi performed using a Korean persona known as Chonangang. SMAP's and Kusanagi's popularity grew throughout Japan, Korea, and China—and so did his style and image.

During a 2001 SMAP concert, Kusanagi performed a segment of the show as Chonangang, "dressed in his trademark pink and white costume, smiling into the camera with dopey eyes and a lipstick-smeared grin."[22] While SMAP's clothing was sometimes quite feminine, with some performances that included cross-dressing, their makeup often used natural-looking coloring, emphasizing smooth skin and soft features, and styled or long hair.

Kusanagi and the other members of SMAP depicted a kind of "soft masculinity" that promoted boyish or androgynous looks and a sensitive, gentle, and nonthreatening nature. This soft masculinity that Kusanagi and others promoted is a kind of opposition to both the violence of Western masculinity ideals and the image of over-worked masculinity in Japan.

The makeup that herbivore men used opened up the possibilities of what masculinity meant. Instead of a life confined to the office and unequal power structures, it indicated a blending of feminine and masculine traits and imagined a future where gentleness and equality in relationships were possible. That pop bands also portrayed a sexuality meant for people attracted to men gave more women, gay men, and gender-nonconforming people a chance to participate in sexual fantasizing in the dominant culture. It meant that women sexualized for a male audience weren't the only representation of sexuality being depicted. These traits were visibly communicated through costuming, including makeup.

Men's use of bolder cosmetics in South Korea and other parts of Asia isn't necessarily a shift toward femininity. Rather, it's recreating masculinity, at times echoing representations of masculinity from history. Historically, certain East Asian cultures have emphasized scholarly learning or political knowledge for their men in leadership positions, so this form of masculinity that emphasized formal knowledge over physical prowess wasn't entirely new. Fukasawa has said that herbivore men were perhaps a return to norm for Japanese men's values, rather than a huge departure.[23] Makeup application can indicate knowing social norms and developing the skills to apply makeup, highlighting emotional knowledge and a gentle hand instead of brute force. Japan and China have also had depictions of pretty young men at times throughout their histories. Historically, makeup has been a tool to help shift the image of masculinity and the ideals it represents by using both more makeup and less or no makeup. Ultimately, these changing expressions of gender help create a new future—a way to change priorities and values from previous generations.

———

Because makeup has become a marker of gender and an indication of gender roles, when people want to expand gender roles and presentation, makeup can lead the way. In the 1970s and '80s in the US and UK, some performers, like David Bowie, Boy George, and Prince, used makeup—along with clothing, performances, and lyrics—to push the boundaries of gender. These performers created new images of masculinity, femininity, and androgyny that allowed their audiences and others to reimagine what gender could be.

When Bowie shot into the mainstream with an appearance of his Ziggy Stardust persona on TV, he changed what masculinity could mean and what it could look like. Ziggy Stardust was an androgynous space alien, sometimes with smudged eyeliner; hollow, contoured cheeks; and lipstick that matched his reddish-orange hair. His skin was pale and iridescent, and to complete the image of otherworldliness, he sometimes painted a metallic circle on his forehead.

When Bowie created personas, makeup and hairstyling were an integral part of his performances. His most recognizable image may be the lightning bolt splayed across his face on the cover of his 1973 album *Aladdin Sane*.[24] Depicted from the shoulders up, Bowie's face is framed by his brilliant orange mullet. A red and blue lightning bolt cuts across half of his face, going from his forehead over his right eye, up over the bridge of his nose, and downward across his cheek. The red of the lightning bolt was drawn on with a shiny red lipstick.[25] His closed eyelids are covered in pink eye shadow. His lashes are thick and black. Pale and dark pink shading on the skin defines his ultra-sharp cheekbones, and his skin almost shines on the high points of his face. His lips are a dusty mauve. His eyebrows seem to disappear under the pale powder or paint that covers his face. This is not masculine or feminine makeup by previous standards. It's something else entirely.

This brightly colored makeup went beyond self-expression to invent a new way of being. It's not a coincidence Ziggy Stardust was imagined as an alien; for many people, defying the gender binary seemed like something normal humans couldn't do. Bowie's makeup helped mainstream culture in the US and UK see a future outside of the gender binary that they may not have imagined before.

Makeup in glam rock and other performance spaces can help stretch boundaries of what's acceptable in public. Some performers choose to wear makeup because it's in violation of gender norms, adding to the rebellious image of their persona that flouts society's rules. Some may wear it because it feels like a truer representation of their own gender. Performance creates a space to play with image that isn't always available in more "professional" office jobs, which typically reinforce gender and class stereotypes. Performance is also an area where pushing boundaries is more tolerated—if it's a performance, it becomes more acceptable than if it were "real life." If something is accepted in a performance, that acceptance can sometimes be relayed into acceptance off the stage. However, performance doesn't protect someone totally from anger or prejudice—Bowie faced threats for wearing a dress while touring in the US in 1971.[26] Fans of Bowie may have faced even more discrimination or danger if they dressed like him or wore bold makeup in the same way and didn't have the protections of wealth and fame.

For new generations, makeup can push gender boundaries even further, both for performers and for civilians. Brightly colored makeup and creative application of makeup have become more accepted for all genders. Gen Z in particular is using makeup to create new ideas of gender presentation, often with the help of social media like YouTube and Instagram.

With the rise of the internet and social media and smartphones that send photos for public and private communication, the importance of the image rose once again in the 2010s, just as it did with the advent of cameras and movies in the mid-1800s and early-to-mid-1900s. For some people, this has translated into an avenue to explore gender presentation—the way Bowie and others have before.

———

On Instagram and other social media platforms, people can create and post makeup looks and connect with others who appreciate the art form. People can also use their makeup to affirm their gender and create new ways of expressing it. While gender-bending with makeup and using makeup to transverse and expand gender roles has always existed, the dominant culture has not always seen or accepted it, and that's beginning to change.

In September 2016, an image that seventeen-year-old James Charles posted of his senior high school photos went viral.[27] When he posted it, Charles wrote that he brought an extra light with him to the photo shoot so that the highlighter on his cheeks would stand out, creating a sharply defined cheekbone. In the image, his light skin appears smooth and unblemished. He has painted freckles artfully dashed across his nose, cheeks, and chin. His thick eyebrows are groomed and combed into place with sharp edges and gaps in his hairs are filled in. They taper to a sharp point. His eyelashes get longer and thicker toward the outer corner of his eye. A white iridescent highlighter powder accentuates the inner corners of his eyes. Highlighter is also placed below and above the arch in his eyebrows, down the center of his nose and on the tip, on top of the cupid's bow on his lips, and on the high point of his cheekbones, which are further defined by shading below the apple of his cheeks. His lips are a soft, muted pink, slightly darker around the edges than the bright center of his bottom lip.

His look encapsulates many mainstream makeup trends in the US of the late 2010s—contouring the cheekbone, highlighter everywhere, thick groomed brows, lips shaded to make them appear thicker, and smooth, perfectly blended, poreless skin. His brows may be thicker than some women's brows, adding a touch of masculinity to makeup trends that are otherwise read as generally feminine in the dominant culture.

On his YouTube channel, Charles presents a variety of makeup looks, from high glam to natural to creative. His makeup isn't bound by gendered rules of what men's makeup or women's makeup should look like. That these looks are shared online allows anyone with internet access to participate by making their own digital runway to show off their made-up face. This digital space becomes a community space where people can trade tips, product recommendations, and ideas. Makeup becomes a tool that helps form a new way to exist, to share, and to create—and anyone of any gender can take part. The makeup looks that people post are not necessarily to be worn outside or to work or school; they are meant to exist only in the image itself. It's a way to reimagine what's possible in a controlled environment with varying levels of risk depending on how someone participates— for example, posting their own photos, commenting, or just viewing others' images.

As makeup is increasingly used by people of all genders, advertisers are capitalizing on this interest. In 2016, CoverGirl named Charles their first male spokesperson. When CoverGirl launched his campaign, Charles had about 650,000 followers on Instagram and 90,000 subscribers to his YouTube channel.[28] In the years since, his channel grew to over 20 million subscribers, as of summer 2020.[29] When asked about his role at CoverGirl, he responded, "Hopefully other people will see this, and when they think, 'Oh, this random 17-year-old kid just started doing makeup recently and is now the face of CoverGirl,' I hope that inspires them to really be themselves and feel comfortable and wear makeup and express themselves in a manner they haven't been comfortable doing before."[30] Charles is an example of anyone, of any gender, picking up a makeup brush and finding skills, creativity, and community and making the life they want. "By putting James, a young Gen Z male, front in center next to the likes of superstars like Katy Perry meant that the beauty industry was betting on boys," wrote David Yi, founder of beauty website Very Good Light, which launched in 2016 and aims to promote an inclusive vision of beauty.[31] Some companies created cosmetic lines specifically for men, once again targeting a gendered group to expand who they can sell to, just as companies did in the early 1900s.

Chanel came out with the line Boy de Chanel in 2018. The products launched first in South Korea, where cosmetics for men are growing significantly, before expanding to be sold worldwide a few months later. The line included three products: lip balm, foundation, and an eyebrow pencil. At the launch, the foundation came in only four shades, limiting the number of people who could use the product and have it match their skin tone. As of 2020, the foundation came in eight shades. (When Fenty launched in 2017, it had forty shades.) Tom Ford Beauty launched a men's grooming line in 2013, and Milk Makeup, formed in 2016, has promoted men's beauty and used models of all genders, among other companies.

"Ultimately, any exposure to men and gender-nonconforming people wearing makeup can only be seen as a step forward, whether a brand's intentions are to move product or challenge gender norms," wrote Bella Cacciatore on Very Good Light.[32] "While using male models will help a brand generate buzz, it will also contribute to the normalization of men using makeup and a less rigid take on gender roles." Their motives may be profit oriented, but seeing billboards with men wearing makeup promoting a legacy brand is still part of reimagining what beauty can be.

However, there is no such thing as makeup for men or women; people of any gender can use the same product. The difference is packaging and marketing. Marketing aggressively to men is still a gendered way to see the world and may just be another way to reinforce gendered differences. Many men who use cosmetics like foundation and eyebrow products often do not even think of them as makeup, especially in certain Asian countries where makeup for men is more popular than in the US. Instead, to appeal to men who previously didn't wear makeup, these cosmetics are reframed as "skin care" or "grooming" products. This framing allows men to wear makeup without calling it makeup—maintaining gendered differences and still leaving makeup for women alone. While this shift may indicate an expansion of masculinity, until makeup becomes divorced from gender entirely, it will still restrict the way some people are able to move through the world.

Gender fluid artist Khai spoke to *Allure* in 2020 about how when they started using makeup, they felt like it might have invalidated their gender. "I knew I loved makeup, but I felt, at first, no one would respect my gender identity if I used it. Now, however, I know I am constantly changing—and so does my makeup," they said.[33] Because makeup was so entrenched in femininity, Khai was concerned about being pigeonholed into womanhood. Instead, they use makeup to express their gender and emphasize that there isn't one way to look any gender.[34]

In one Instagram post, Khai has thick black lip liner and shading on their lips, with neon yellow on the center of their full bottom lip.[35] Yellow powder also appears on their eyes, going from the corner of the eye outward, in a lightning-bolt shape reminiscent of Bowie, but yellow with a black outline and symmetrical on both eyes. Their eyelashes are yellow too, and tiny lightning bolts appear in their hair. In another post, their lips and eyelids are covered in pink glitter, with light blue powder across the brow bone.[36] Their eyebrows are pink, and glitter highlighter covers their brown skin. In another, a white snake eating its tail is drawn in a figure eight around their eyes, with white eyelashes and thick, groomed brows to complete the look.[37] In their Instagram bio, they have the word "shapeshifter" to let people know they "shouldn't project any one look as my entire identity," they said.[38] Using social media to portray a huge variety of intricate and creative makeup looks expands what gender presentation can be. This, in turn, expands what life can be like for people of all genders. With more freedom to look different and have that appearance not tied to any gender, the freedom to live outside of the gender binary can follow.

When comic artist Matt Lubchansky came out as genderqueer, lipstick helped them affirm their gender. They had worn nail polish and earrings before. But to them, lipstick was something "inescapably femme" that they could wear to assert themselves. "We talk a lot about gender identity as something innate, unchosen. And it's true—you don't choose to feel this way," they wrote in a comic in 2018. "But there's something lost in that discussion. If the identity you're told you have isn't the one that fits, you do have to make a choice. To change what other people see."[39] Lipstick was something Lubchansky felt could portray their genderqueerness. Lipstick is a tool that sometimes reinforces the gender binary—but as Lubchansky shows, it can also help break it.

Throughout much of history, makeup has been a way to reinforce gendered appearances and ideals—but that hasn't always been the case and it doesn't have to be in the future. Experimenting with makeup can actually help people divest of the gender binary and the idea that appearance and gender have to be related at all. Presenting a certain way isn't a requirement for any gender, but it can help people to create a new space for how they can live in the world. As new generations are showing on social media and in real life, the visual medium of makeup can be a way to experiment and play with gender—or a way to just play, without worrying about gender at all.

SAFETY NOT GUARANTEED

Content Warning: Some readers may find aspects of the following chapter upsetting.

People protected by the dominant culture can often move through the world without thinking about it. This includes able-bodied cisgender white men and thin white women with long straight hair especially. Their appearance is protected by society's expectation that they have a right to exist in public spaces. For others who don't fall under this protection—anyone disabled, people who cross gender boundaries, and people of color, for example—appearance can be fraught. Breaking from appearance norms, including norms around grooming and personal presentation, can lead to ridicule, harassment, and violence. Learning to blend in with others can be a skill one develops as a survival tactic to minimize the harm of living without the support from people and institutions that others automatically receive.

Writer and activist Janet Mock wrote in her memoir *Redefining Realness* that as she was growing up, she experienced sharp differences in how people treated her depending on how she looked. Mock was assigned male at birth, and when she was younger, she attempted to suppress her femininity for a time to appear to conform to strict

gender roles and avoid teasing and harassment that came from defying gendered expectations. "Mom never asked me to butch up; I just
did it, and the world reacted differently. I noticed a shift in how other
kids treated me," she wrote.[1] Mock tried to shield herself from harm
and bullying by presenting as a boy that fit into masculine ideals that
rejected femininity in any form. For her, that meant no makeup, no
dresses, and short hair. As Mock transitioned, she found that fitting into feminine ideals while presenting as a woman also provided
protection from harassment or harm. "As my body began evolving,
the world treated me differently, and I learned firsthand that society
privileges physical beauty," Mock wrote.[2]

For trans women, makeup can be a signal to society that affirms
their gender because of gendered expectations that women wear
makeup. "Yet while makeup's benefits may be a universal aspect of
womanhood, for trans women, 'failing' at makeup can have much
higher stakes," wrote Lux Alptraum in a 2017 article for Racked titled
"Makeup Can Give Trans Women Freedom—But It Can Also Take
It Away." Using makeup can help trans women avoid harassment and
assault, get and keep jobs, and even help be approved for certain medical procedures that require the recipient to show proof of "living as a
woman."[3] Even though many women don't wear makeup, cisgender
women don't need to outwardly prove their womanhood for the world
to accept it. Makeup is a relatively cost-effective way for trans women
to transform their appearance and to affirm their womanhood to other
people. "Cosmetics may not make the woman, but using cosmetics
makes being read as a woman easier," Alptraum wrote.[4] Foundation
can hide stubble on the face, highlighting can soften certain features,
contour can create shadows to slim and define cheekbones or foreheads, and lipstick can change the shape of the lip to fit beauty ideals
based on cisgender women. "And when not being read as a woman
means harassment, unemployment, assault, and even death, makeup
goes from being optional to being essential," she wrote.

To learn how to wear makeup, Mock went to the MAC Cosmetics counter at a department store in Hawaii with her friend Wendi,

who is also a trans woman. The people working at the MAC counter made Mock feel welcome to experiment with her look—which isn't guaranteed for customers shopping for makeup who don't fit into the gender binary or who don't fit into strict societal expectations about how women should look. In 1994, MAC had hired cisgender male Black drag queen RuPaul to advertise its Viva Glam lipstick, and 100 percent of the proceeds went to the MAC AIDS Fund. The company has prioritized employing and serving those who don't fit into straight, white beauty ideals, and for Mock and her friend, the makeup counter allowed them to safely experiment with makeup and femininity. Mock wrote that Wendi tweezed Mock's eyebrows into a thin curve and reassured Mock when she wore silver eye shadow to school. When the girls in Mock's class complimented her makeup, she smiled at the positive attention she received.[5]

A safe space to explore gender and appearance in public, like the MAC counter for Mock, is rare. People who are trans or gender nonconforming may not have a safe way to experiment with makeup and their appearance. Their families may not approve of experimentation at home, which could lead to ostracism and abuse, and in public, the risk of harassment or violence may be high for people who don't conform to gendered expectations.

———

What is safe and accepted in the dominant culture can also change over time. In the 1920s in the US, prohibition began to blur what was socially acceptable as normally law-abiding people gathered in speakeasies and other illicit places to drink. In this environment, flamboyant and effeminate gay men known as pansies used makeup like lipstick to flout expectations of masculinity. This style spread to other cities in the US and Europe. However, after the Great Depression took hold and World War II began, culture shifted again, and the dominant culture used this lipstick as a way to condemn those who were LGBTQ. In Berlin, many popular pansies were sent to the concentration camps of Nazi Germany, where they were killed.[6]

In the US, LGBTQ subcultures were forced back underground, and blending in with the dominant culture was a method for survival. In director Jennie Livingston's documentary *Paris Is Burning*, about the LGBTQ ball scene in New York in the late 1980s, trans woman and drag queen Dorian Corey describes "realness" as being able to "pass to the untrained eye—or even the trained eye—and not give away the fact that you're gay."[7] For someone who is transgender, passing means not being visibly trans. However, as Mock writes, "If a trans woman who knows herself and operates in the world as a woman is seen, perceived, treated, and viewed as a woman, isn't she just being herself? She isn't *passing*; she is merely *being*."[8]

In *Paris Is Burning*, Corey puts the idea of realness in context of being able to safely move through the world when she says, "When they're undetectable—when they can walk out of that ballroom into the sunlight and onto the subway and get home and still have all their clothes and no blood running off their bodies—those are the femme realness queens."[9] In the ball scene, realness was also an art form, and one of the categories where people could compete in a type of pageant. In the rest of the world, realness could act as a shield that provided some protection when a woman left the LGBTQ safe space of the ball and entered the wider city.

According to Transgender Europe, an advocacy and research organization started in 2005, from January 2008 through September 30, 2018, in seventy-two countries, 2,982 trans or gender-nonconforming people were reported murdered.[10] For many countries there is limited information available, so that number is likely larger. In the US, most of those murdered—85 percent—were people of color. For the victims whose occupations were known, over half were sex workers. Many trans women who have been sex workers weren't able to get other employment because of discrimination that kept them from being hired—or because they were fired or forced out of jobs because of their gender. Working as a sex worker as a teenager, Mock wrote, she "learned to use my beauty as currency to get the things I needed. I no longer had to rely on Mom for the medicine. I became my sole provider of my hormones, my clothes, my makeup, and my hair appointments."[11] The money she made from sex work gave her independence and control over her life—and her appearance. This independence allowed Mock to provide herself with the care she needed, and having control over her appearance gave her freedom and stability.

Mock's appearance as a beautiful woman had other advantages as well. She wrote about what she calls "pretty privilege" for *Allure* in 2017. She describes it as the societal advantages, often unearned, that people receive when others consider them beautiful. "Pretty privilege is also conditional and is not often extended to women who are trans, black and brown, disabled, older, and/or fat," she wrote.[12] Mock is a Black woman, and though she experiences pretty privilege in certain places, racism often attempts to keep Black women from being accepted into dominant culture's beauty standards. In addition, transphobia often attempts to exclude transgender people from being seen as pretty.

Sometimes makeup used to make someone appear more feminine—and therefore "pretty" as the dominant culture defines it—hides or downplays physical traits that are associated with masculinity, like facial hair stubble and a sharp jawline. Makeup artist and feminine image consultant Monica Prata shared makeup tips for trans women with BuzzFeed in 2016, including using a makeup brush to stipple full coverage foundation into the parts of the face where facial hair grows.[13] Prata also suggested blending makeup that's a shade or two darker than a woman's skin on the outer edges of the face to contour and make the face appear slimmer. Overdrawing lipstick and accentuating the cupid's bow on the upper lip can create the appearance of fuller lips.

Cisgender people often use these same makeup tricks to put together their appearance and call attention to or minimize certain features of their face. But when trans people use these techniques, cis people may wield them as evidence that trans women are creating a mask to "deceive" others. "Cis men have often claimed that they were 'deceived' or 'tricked' by a trans woman who was assumed to be cis and was thereby deserving of the violence she faced," Mock wrote. The same makeup that trans women may use to blend in with the dominant culture and stay safer could become a risk to wear in other circumstances.

For trans women, passing and pretty privilege are not guarantees of safety. In *Paris Is Burning*, drag queen and trans woman Venus Xtravaganza discussed the features she believed helped her make the most money as a sex worker: her petiteness, blond hair, light skin, green eyes, and small features.[14] These features are also ones that help her fit into the dominant culture's beauty ideals. When she speaks into the camera, her thin eyebrows arch over her eyes, which are rimmed with black eyeliner. Her lips are shiny and pink with a gloss or lipstick. Venus tells the story of a time when she was working as a sex worker and a client discovered she was trans. The man accused her of being crazy and of trying to give him AIDS, and he threatened to kill her. Venus was able to escape out a window. However, at the end of the film, it's revealed that Venus was found murdered, strangled in a hotel room.[15] The details around her death aren't known, but it's implied that a client may have killed her.

The violent client and the person who murdered Venus are examples of violence trans women can face. If looking feminine—as defined by the dominant culture based on cisgender bodies—can become a way to stay safer and move more easily through the world, then maintaining appearances becomes rigidly necessary for survival. But makeup alone doesn't protect trans women from harassment or violence. Even when trans women are not visibly trans, harm can still follow. Makeup can be one tool trans women use depending on their situation to attempt to provide an extra layer of protection, but it doesn't guarantee safety in a world that punishes being transgender.

The harm that comes to women when they don't fit into certain beauty ideals doesn't always look like harassment or violence. It could be prejudice, withholding services, or systemic injustice built into the systems society uses to function. In Chicago in the 1920s, a string of women arrested for murder was covered heavily in newspapers and on the radio, reflecting a seeming increase in crime as the city was coping with the speakeasies and gangster activity that prohibition wrought. This increase in publicized woman-led violent crime attracted spectators who were fascinated with the idea of women murderers—though not all who were arrested were convicted of their crimes.

The accused women were housed together at Cook County Jail in what became known as Murderess Row. There, they discovered that the city's court system favored white women who used makeup to look wealthy and beautiful. Women who didn't fit the ultrafeminized, beautiful image of a modern woman—with short bobbed hair styled with Marcel curls, a fashionable hat, groomed thin eyebrows, and dark lipstick—were seen as animalistic, villainous, and murderous. Women who fit the pretty image of a wealthy or made-up woman went free.

Italian immigrant Sabella Nitti was one of the women arrested and sent to Cook County Jail. She was charged with killing her husband, Francesco Nitti, who disappeared from their farm one night in the summer of 1922 after an argument with their son, apparently taking with him the family's $300 of savings. Evidence pointing to his wife as a killer was sparse, but police arrested her for the crime after a body—but not necessarily his body—was discovered in a catch basin. Because Sabella Nitti was a poor immigrant who didn't speak English, and because she didn't fit into the dominant culture's idea of a "proper" (wealthy) lady, she became an easy mark for law enforcement. At the time, the court system was aiming to sentence a woman to death for the first time in Cook County's history because those in power in Chicago wanted to give the impression that the city would be just as hard on female killers as it was on male killers.[16]

In addition, Chicago's court systems had acquitted several accused women murderers, and the story that the city was soft on beautiful women took hold in the public consciousness.

In a picture of Nitti in the *Chicago Daily Tribune* from the end of her trial, she sits slouching, with her chin in her hand and her grey hair pulled high on her head. Her face is tilted downward, and her clothing appears to be made of rough cotton. In another small image, Nitti's unsmiling face is framed by thick eyebrows.[17] To try to win the court case and achieve his goal of convicting Nitti, the prosecutor built his case around the way she looked, using sexist and racist stereotypes to try to convince the jury she had killed her husband with the help of her hired farmhand. Nitti had long hair, rather than the trendy short bob haircut of the 1920s. She wore shabby clothing and used carpet squares for shoes. And she didn't wear makeup. "Can you see that woman? No. She isn't a woman, she is a fiend, she is not a woman," the prosecutor Milton Smith said during Nitti's trial.[18] Smith's words give away what many men in Chicago thought at the time—that a woman was supposed to be beautiful, and that the absence of beauty meant the absence of womanhood. Even in a supposedly modern city like Chicago, the conventional idea of womanhood at the time meant that women were nurturing instead of violent, soft instead of harsh, and weak instead of strong. Because Nitti didn't fit into popular beauty conventions for wealthy white women, the prosecutor painted her as a savage, violent person, and it was easier for the white men who made up juries in Illinois to believe she had done something wrong. They found Nitti guilty, and she was sentenced to death.

When the jury read the verdict, *Chicago Daily Tribune* reporter Genevieve Forbes wrote that "Mrs. Nitti ran stubby fingers, where the dirt was ingrained into broken nails into her matted hair. She shifted her stocky legs and smoothed out the dark blue skirt, made full and short for work in the field. She hadn't understood a word. But she twisted up her face in a grotesque angle of fear, and inferiocity, and cruelty and hope." She also wrote that Nitti was a "dumb, crouching, animal-like Italian peasant."[19] Forbes's racism reflected that of the people in the courtroom and on the jury, and these harmful views supported the court system in its prosecution of Nitti.

In truth, Nitti couldn't communicate well with those around her, didn't understand what was happening to her, and in all likelihood didn't actually kill her husband. When Nitti's appeal process started, she worked with a lawyer who changed her fate. A lawyer named Helen Cirese was among those who took up Nitti's case, and she made some changes to the way Nitti looked in an effort to change the story being told about her. Cirese and her colleagues founded the Justinian Society of Lawyers, a professional group of Chicago-based Italian American lawyers, in 1921. They understood what it was like to be discriminated against based on their heritage, and Cirese in particular knew what it was like to fight to be taken seriously as a woman. She couldn't get hired by law firms around the city because of her gender, so she started her own practice. Nitti was one of her first clients.

She and the other lawyers helped Nitti navigate appeals, but perhaps just as importantly, Cirese got Nitti new clothes, dyed her hair, and taught her English. Cirese and another woman, Margaret Borelli, brought hair dye to the jail for Nitti to color her hair a trendy dark brown or black. Borelli also helped Nitti learn American mannerisms and to speak and write some English. Forbes wrote that Nitti used lemon juice to lighten her skin and that, in jail, she was able to bathe regularly.[20] These superficial changes were an attempt to make Nitti seem more conventional and familiar to the lawyers, judge, and jury working on her case and to transform her into the stereotypical image of a nonviolent "proper" woman.

After her makeover, Nitti's hair looked shiny and dark, perfectly curled and cropped to frame her face. Her eyebrows were dark to match her hair and formed a thin, plucked arch over her eyes. In one photo, she smiled, turning her face youthful, as she held up an example of her writing in English. The light gleamed off of her lips, which were darkened with lipstick.[21] "When she walked into that courtroom she was beautiful—beautiful and innocent. I'll never forget how she looked," Cirese said.[22] By following popular makeup trends like thin eyebrows and lipstick, Nitti's makeup helped her blend in with the upper-class society that was judging her.

This new look, and the coverage of it in the newspapers, helped the public see Nitti as someone who could be innocent. Her case garnered public support, and Nitti was eventually granted a retrial from the Illinois Supreme Court. She was later released on bail, and without any additional evidence, her trial kept getting pushed back until it was dropped entirely.

Another woman's experience on Murderess Row illustrates how the court system worked if one entered it with the advantage of the appearance of wealth and glamour. Belva Gaertner was accused of murdering her married boyfriend, Walter Law. Gaertner was wealthier and more fashionably dressed than Nitti—after her arrest, she was worried about cleaning blood off of her expensive wool coat, and she used a powder puff to reapply her makeup.[23] Her expertise in fashion and makeup indicated to others she had a wealthy lifestyle that emphasized her femininity as a white woman. Her appearance made it hard for the white male jurors and the rest of the dominant culture outside the courtroom to believe she was capable of murder—even though, unlike Nitti, there was evidence she did kill Law. Instead, it was easier for the men to believe that a woman like Gaertner fell in love and got caught up in her emotions, leading her into a troubled situation where someone ended up dead.

A few newspapers showed how this storyline could take precedence over the truth. Newspapers from the Hearst company often retouched photos of accused woman murderers to make them appear more beautiful, according to strict beauty standards that focused on young, thin, white women. The newspapers painted out wrinkles and under-eye circles, making older women appear younger and haggard women more vivacious. This built a storyline of glamour gone wrong, advertising drama for the public to consume. "With their emphasis on sensation and sentimentality, the Hearst newspapers had a stake in their murderesses looking more beautiful than those in the staid *Tribune* and *Daily News*, and their artists competed with each other like rival funeral-home directors," wrote Douglas Perry in *The Girls of Murder City*.[24] In turn, these beautiful images granted these women a cloak of support from the public, who found their beauty alluring. This helped women like Gaertner automatically get the support that Nitti had to work so hard to receive.

After Nitti's trial, the women in the jail saw what happened to a woman on trial for her life who didn't maintain certain beauty trends. The women in Cook County Jail began talking with each other about what to wear to their trials, often with help from Gaertner, who was considered knowledgeable about beauty and fashion. The women on Murderess Row had access to a makeup cabinet filled with cosmetics confiscated from women who came into the jail. Items in the cabinet may have included things like cake mascara, which was invented in 1913 by T. L. Williams, the founder of Maybelline. Likely dark lipsticks would be available after they became popular in the 1920s because of actresses like Theda Bara and Madge Bellamy. Vaseline also may have been used to make eyelids shiny, giving the face a soft angelic glow.

The women were allowed to use what they wanted from the cabinet on the days of their trials. In a 1927 article headlined "Jail Can Really Do a Lot for a Woman," Forbes wrote that Nitti became an "outstanding graduate of the jail school" after she turned her cell into a "'salon de beaute,' and she worked overtime at this business of making herself fair." Forbes said she came into the jail a "horrible looking creature," and left a "butterfly" with "rouge on her cheeks."[25] Forbes's words drew on other stereotypes based on women's looks, framing Nitti as narcissistic and obsessed with her new beauty routine, which she didn't have access to outside of jail because she was poor. A reporter for the *Post* wrote, "Hers is probably one of the few cases on record where it has been established beyond all doubt that long confinement behind bars did the prisoner any good."[26] These reporters seemed to equate a woman's stylish appearance with improved well-being. But Nitti's new look wasn't for her personal pleasure; it was to help her get control of her case and keep her from the death penalty.

There was a perception that a beautiful woman wouldn't get convicted in Chicago. To ignore that was to go into a trial that your life depended on at a disadvantage. If these women didn't take control of their looks, that just allowed someone else—like Nitti's prosecutor—to take control of their story. They got dressed up and made up to impress the jury the way some women tried to woo a man on a date. And since juries consisted of all white men, likely with fairly similar cultural ideas of womanhood, this strategy seemed to work.

Dressing for court wasn't just about appearing wealthy or beautiful—though that was certainly part of it for these women. It was more about changing their appearances to make themselves and their stories familiar to the jury: a love story gone wrong, instead of a person capable of committing cold-hearted violence. The women on trial understood that they needed to appear like they couldn't be violent and maybe needed rescuing. They also needed to look slightly seductive, so it would make sense they got caught up in something that had gotten out of hand. A beautiful woman who fell into a violent situation or who needed to perform self-defense was a story that made sense to a jury. These feelings were born from stereotypes that a woman who was seductive couldn't help but get into trouble that could escalate beyond her control—thus was the power and attraction of her beauty. The women on Murderess Row tried to create an image that paired that seductiveness with respectability, purity, and innocence.

———

For women who are victims of crimes instead of accused of committing them, appearance can be an equally important tool in the court system. For victims, image may be used to emphasize attributes like honor and stability. For rape survivors, makeup can be an especially valuable tool to use in a trial where image and reputation may take on outsized importance. A woman complainant in a rape trial may use her appearance to come across as trustworthy, chaste, and responsible—and therefore not someone who could have invented a story to save face or garner attention, as prosecutors often attempt to argue. Instead of following beauty trends like Nitti, a complainant may want to wear conservative makeup to indicate she is a sensible and conscientious person. This image can help rape survivors navigate the justice system where so few rape cases end up—and where even fewer end with a conviction.

Willingness to appear in court is a key component of the prosecution of rape, wrote sociologist Amanda Konradi. In the process of going to trial, including pretrial court events, rape survivors will see their assailants in person and be seen themselves by prosecutors, juries, and judges. What goes into preparing for these events depends on the survivor's experience with the legal system, class, and goals, Konradi writes. But one aspect of preparation for a trial appears to remain consistent across the board; that is, a survivor must consider how to present herself to the jury. As part of their preparations to appear in court or court-related events, women participated in what Konradi calls "appearance work." In a study, Konradi spoke with thirty-two women who testified as part of the prosecution of their rape cases. Of the women in the study, 29 percent said they tried to achieve a demeanor that was "consistent with idealized images of witnesses or victims."[27] Konradi wrote that the survivors in her study talked about purposefully creating an image that "conformed with visual standards separating real victims from women 'who asked for it.'"[28] This persona was "conservative, businesslike, and nonsexual," and so women chose clothes that hid their bodies and kept their makeup minimal.

One woman said she wore a little lipstick, and another said waterproof mascara was a "necessity item." While the waterproofing might have been necessary to avoid smudged makeup during an emotional trial, mascara could have also been needed because of the way it can transform the face. Mascara can be used to create a variety of different effects around the eyes—from thick layers to create a sense of glamour and sex appeal to a lighter brush for a softer, more youthful look—but generally speaking, longer lashes have the effect of making the eyes seem larger. Evidence suggests that humans tend to warm toward other adults with childlike features, such as large eyes or full lips, in the same way some people instinctively want to care for a child. Research around faces with immature-looking facial features—such as those that may resemble a child or baby—shows that onlookers may judge people with these features to be "weak, submissive, helpless, dependent, feminine, and warm."[29] From this perspective, the impulse to wear mascara to a trial makes a lot of sense. Childlike eyes can be a beacon of innocence, with wide eyes acting as a plea for help.

Women often can't rely on seeming authoritative or strong to make a point because they are punished in a society that associates gentleness with women and strength with men. In a rape trial, women often must prove that they made it clear they did not consent by proving their "goodness and niceness." Often, portraying sexual purity is key in this process. During trials, women complainants have been asked if they were single mothers, if they smoked or drank, and if they wore false eyelashes and red lipstick.[30] As discussed in the sexuality chapter, makeup can portray an image of sexuality, and bold makeup, like red lipstick, can be associated with sex and romance—and that image can hurt women in court in a rape trial.

A woman's choice of cosmetics can also be weaponized by others who are attempting to discredit her—just as with Sabella Nitti before her makeover. In addition, prosecutors may decide whether to pursue a case based on whether they believe they could get a conviction. This could mean that a woman's chances of obtaining legal representation rely on her ability to make herself up as credible—even to the lawyer she's relying on to help her tell her story.

Many subjective assumptions go into assessing someone's credibility, including ones based on racism, classism, and sexism. A perceived lack of femininity and chastity makes working-class women less credible as rape victims, writes Alison Phipps.[31] Respectability and femininity are defined by what they are measured against, and often that's working-class women. "Rape trials generally turn on the issue of consent, and it seems that this is inversely linked to respectability, since those who fail to meet the respectability criterion are thought to have permanent consent to sexual violation written into their behaviour," Phipps wrote.[32] Because rape trials often hinge on the reputations of the victim and the accused, perceptions around class and sexuality can make a difference in court. The makeup a survivor wears can be a marker of class, with heavier makeup indicating a violation of what the upper class often deems as "proper" and less overtly sexual.

There is a harmful stereotype that a woman who is sexual is a risk-taker who will put herself in harm's way, therefore becoming partly responsible for the violence that occurred. In one rape trial in Ireland in 2018, a defense lawyer talking about the claimant told a jury, "You have to look at the way she was dressed. She was wearing a thong with a lace front."[33] A woman's underwear became evidence of her sexuality and that she had been trying to attract someone. In that trial, the man accused of raping her went free, demonstrating how pervasive the belief is that a sexual woman won't say no to sex at any time. Knowing this, the women in Konradi's study thought about how their appearances would represent them as victims, and they used makeup to try to fit the image of a "model victim" to try to support their case.

Wearing makeup has no effect on whether a woman will be assaulted, but it does have an effect on whether that woman will see justice in a courtroom. Women chase respectability—often just out of reach—using tools like makeup because they are trying to work within a system that doesn't value their bodily autonomy or self-worth without a polished veneer. This shield of femininity can help provide protection and justice, but it also traps women inside. If woman doesn't fit into the image that others have of what a woman "should" be, she will likely face greater trouble in institutions built on supporting gendered expectations and upholding the status quo. And by selecting cases that they expect will receive convictions based in part on a woman's appearance, prosecutors support and reinforce the same system that leaves some women without a chance for justice or protection.

The persona that some women create to appear as a "model victim" is often a safer way to traverse the court system at the time, but it hides the nuances of trauma and truth beneath a made-up veneer, which could lead to lasting harm. A woman at a trial may become a flattened character, using her makeup to portray an image of innocence and purity that no real woman could live up to. This image reinforces the myth of perfect victims and leads women to be trapped within the stereotype they are portraying, disappearing under the image they create.

Outside of the courtroom, women use makeup, or a pointed lack of makeup, to disappear under stereotypes in other ways. An Allied spy named Christine Granville's particular strength was her ability to manipulate her appearance to render herself invisible in any social milieu. She anticipated others' assumptions and created an image of herself that fit easily into a narrative that suited her purpose. When she needed to sneak by a Nazi in the Alps, she created a dull-faced version of herself with no makeup and tied-back hair to blend in with innocent local women. Conversely, when she needed to sneak documents across country borders, possibly while traveling from Austria to Poland, she made herself up as a flirtatious young woman, "dressed in fresh clothes, hair washed, lips painted," and was able to fool a Gestapo officer into carrying the documents in his luggage so they wouldn't be discovered.[34] The ability to navigate different appearances depending on the situation helped her keep her cover, saving her life and her mission as she interacted with German soldiers. Granville either hid behind glamour or became unworthy of arousing suspicion because of a lack of it. Both kept her safe. Women can also use this invisibility to get access to places and experiences they otherwise wouldn't be allowed by promoting a frivolous and feminine look that hides the seriousness within. This plays on sexist expectations that beautiful made-up women can't be smart or care about worldly topics like politics or war, and women spies have often used this assumption to their advantage.

Born in Missouri, Josephine Baker traveled to France when she was cast in La Revue Nègre, which opened in 1925. In Paris, Baker became famous for a performance of an erotic dance, wearing not much more than a skirt decorated with artificial bananas. In her "banana-skirted jungle dance," Baker, a Black woman, subverted tropes of African primitiveness, and audiences became enamored with her dancing and image of wild sexuality.[35]

Baker made a living as an entertainer in part because of her beautiful appearance, which she cultivated to capitalize on blending in with trends and knowing when to subvert them. In a picture of Baker from Getty Images taken around 1928, her short black hair is shellacked and shiny, lying flat on her head. Her eyes are circled and smudged with a smoky dark shadow, topped by her thin dark eyebrows. Her gentle eyebrow arch mirrors the swipe of her eye shadow, which glistens, drawing attention from onlookers. Her shadow extends past the outer corner of her eye toward her temple, making her eyes a prominent feature on her face—and her audience was enthralled to look into them. Her smile is painted with dark lipstick, and her smooth, flawless skin portrays youth.[36] Her makeup indicated a modern woman who was independent and went after what she wanted; flappers had the reputation of flouting conventions that kept women at home and devoted to domesticity. Baker's appearance also drew attention to her sexuality by portraying a glamorous image with heavy makeup that one might wear to a nightclub. She emphasized her sexuality in her performances to help her create star appeal. Underneath her sexuality was a canny performer who knew how to enthrall audiences with both her physicality and her witty personality.

Over the years, Baker's renown grew, and her singing and dancing made her a famous entertainer in Europe. Her beauty, which was well publicized, helped her become famous—for example, she was paid to be in advertisements for Valaze Water Lily beauty cream, which claimed, "You can have a body like Joséphine Baker if you use Valaze cream."[37]

But it was Baker's strength of character, in addition to her ability to use her beauty as a ticket into exclusive clubs and parties, that made her an asset to the Allies during World War II. Early on in the war, France's military intelligence Le Deuxième Bureau looked to recruit people who could move around freely and gather information about the war—informants they called honorable correspondents. An acquaintance recommended Baker to a military officer named Jacques Abtey. Abtey was at first suspicious of using women as spies, believing stereotypes that women were unreliable and prone to wanting romance over duty to country. He was especially wary of Baker, who he heard was eccentric and sexual, which was part of the persona she promoted as a dancer and an artist.[38]

Baker recognized German Nazis for what they were: racist and fascist. After Kristallnacht in November 1938, when Nazis in Germany and Austria set fire to Jewish homes, stores, and synagogues and attacked Jewish people in the streets, Baker publicly joined the International League Against Racism and Anti-Semitism. Years earlier she had publicly supported Benito Mussolini after he allowed her to perform in Italy, and she had fallen for his "strength of personality," believing he would help end slavery in Ethiopia, which Italy invaded in 1935.[39] The occurrence of Kristallnacht indicated a shift in her priorities and a greater understanding of the risks of fascist politics, and her public stand against Nazism indicated the bravery Baker possessed. The acquaintance who introduced Baker to Abtey recommended her in part because of her courage. Baker was also devoted to her adopted country of France. When she met

Abtey, she claimed that France made her what she was; she had given her heart to the people of Paris and she was willing to give her life to them as well.

Impressed by her patriotism and charm, Abtey hired Baker as an honorable correspondent in spite of his initial doubts. Baker was to use her numerous social contacts to attend parties and learn information that could be helpful to France, like the location of German troops. Her unfortunate remarks in support of Mussolini years earlier had granted her an open invitation to the Italian Embassy, and Abtey was eager to learn information about Italy joining the war. Baker was charming, brave, and devoted to the cause, willing to take risks to help others. The same reasons Abtey was wary of using Baker for intelligence gathering were the reasons why she was a particularly good choice for a spy: her appearance made her seem frivolous and unimportant, more interested in flirting than the war. She had social contacts who were presumably happy to drink with a pretty girl and who didn't believe she could be a vital part of the war effort.

When some people looked at a flapper or a performer, all they saw was a woman who cared for pleasure and nothing else. But Baker was practical in a crisis. After the German army occupied Paris, Baker loaded her car with all the supplies she could—along with her maid and two refugees—and drove to southern France. She knew that gas could be difficult to find on the journey, so she filled some champagne bottles with gasoline.[40] Like Baker herself, the frivolity and sparkle of the outward appearance of the champagne bottles hid practicality and resourcefulness within.

During World War II, people in Europe faced difficulties in gathering visas required to travel between countries. Because of her fame and her role as an entertainer, Baker had an easier time than others getting the papers she needed. Her performances provided a legitimate reason for traveling, and her fame and beauty provided a smoke screen of glamour that few questioned. She was also able to leverage her fame to get documents to help other people get places or help the Allied cause.

Baker often hid or disguised messages to transport the information she discovered. In one instance, she traveled with information written in invisible ink in the margins of her sheet music.[41] In another, she took notes of what she overheard at parties and pinned the information to her underwear.[42] As she said, "Who would dare search Josephine Baker to the skin?"[43] Her beauty gave her access to valuable spaces—like parties where sensitive information was discussed—then it provided a shield to transport information safely away. Baker's appearance was a calculated front that helped her achieve stardom—and her ability to hide her intentions under that image of stardom, depending on her goals, was a skill she developed to keep herself and her country safer.

In many situations, makeup becomes a way for women to have agency over what happens to them, which may help keep them safer. But the shield of femininity that makeup can help create is a product of sexist systems that don't protect all women. Using makeup as protection by playing upon society's views of harmless femininity can be effective. But it can also mean that people become stuck within those conventions and that women who don't fit into those conventions don't receive the same support. In this case, makeup is a tool the way a parachute is a tool—it may be a choice to wear it, but what happens when someone goes without it?

TOO FEW SHADES

M akeup can be an important tool to navigate safety and the workplace, among many other everyday uses, but for a long time in the US modern makeup was not widely available to women of color. Modern cosmetic manufacturers operated under the racist assumption that Black women could never want to be beautiful, and most companies saw white women as their customers. Even today, makeup made for people of color is less accessible than makeup made in shades to match white skin. While racism and colorism in a beauty industry that prefers light skin is apparent in many places around the world, the US has a particular history with racism in the beauty industry.

In the US, physical traits of enslaved people—like dark skin or dark, textured hair—were seen as ways to distinguish enslaved men and women from those who were free. White people who were in power viewed people with light or white skin as more valuable to society than those with dark skin. The dominant class of wealthier white people has reinforced these superficial physical traits throughout history as a means of maintaining control, legally and socially, over people of color.[1] Skin color and other physical traits associated with Black people were visible ways to make distinctions between people, reinforce social and economic hierarchies, and maintain power structures that kept Black people out. White people used beauty standards they set as a way to keep Black and brown people from the social and economic capital that could come from being viewed as stylish or beautiful.

At some plantations in the antebellum US, enslaved people were not allowed to do certain things that plantation owners deemed too African, which included wrapping or braiding their hair, playing drums, or engaging in religious practices.[2] In addition, enslaved people generally didn't have access to hygiene products or time to spend on grooming practices like hair care, and enslavers would mock efforts of personal grooming. As a result, Black women in slavery weren't able to pass on how to properly care for their hair. For these women and their descendants, this lost knowledge of hygiene practices, especially around care for Black hair, sometimes resulted in scalp disease, with hair falling out or being unable to grow.

The fact that slavery denied Black people the option of practicing any real hygienic or beauty routines made it easy for white people to claim superior hygiene for themselves. White people used hair and other beauty trends as standards to separate Black and white people. In short, white people kept Black people from participating in hair care or styling, then white people used this to create a social narrative where white people were perceived as "clean" and "beautiful" and Black people were described as "brutes" and "ugly" in newspapers and other media. This narrative was reinforced via advertisements for beauty products targeted exclusively at white people's hair, implying that only white people could hope to achieve beauty. Media stories further illustrated that preferred beauty standards were based on white bodies—even children's books and toys, like the Golliwog books based on a rag doll that looked like a minstrel character and Hugh Lofting's *Doctor Dolittle* books, which included an African prince who wished his skin were white.

White women's naturally straight and shiny hair was marketed toward Black women as the look to achieve, while Black women were socially punished for having textured hair that didn't conform to that standard. Differences in hair care and styling were also used in Black communities to separate upper- and middle-class Black people from the poor and uneducated, who didn't have the money or knowledge to groom their hair a certain way. In these ways and more, beauty techniques and hairstyles were used to reinforce white supremacy, keeping white people separate from Black people and visually reinforcing white people's higher social and economic class.

Structural discrimination and individual prejudices further prevented Black women from participating in beauty and fashion trends by denying them access to stores where makeup and clothing were sold. In the late 1800s, Black women in the US were not allowed to work on the sales floor in department stores and could only shop in some department stores, depending on the state. In some places, Black women were allowed to shop if they were wearing their maid uniform and had a list written by their employer.[3] In addition, department stores refused to sell beauty products marketed to Black women. It was rules like these that drove Black business owners like Anthony Overton, who started a cosmetic company in 1898, and Madam C. J. Walker, who founded her hair-care and cosmetics company in 1906, to sell door-to-door to Black customers, instead of in brick-and-mortar stores.

Madam Walker knew that hair care, personal grooming, and skin color were tied to financial gains for Black women. Looking clean and professional may help anyone get a job, but Black women are especially pressured to look "respectable." This is problematic because the standard of respectability is set by the dominant—white—culture, and white folks tend to favor traits that resemble their own, resulting in workplace customs and expectations that actively discriminate against people of color. Moreover, there were few grooming products marketed to Black folks. Madam Walker saw that this deficit, combined with unattainable aesthetic standards and discrimination, contributed to the larger trend of Black unemployment during this period in American history after the Civil War.

Madam Walker knew Black women were judged more harshly than white women when it came to their appearance and saw how this affected employment, so another part of her business goal was helping Black women achieve financial independence. She did this in part by teaching grooming practices to help Black women prevent scalp disease and help hair grow. She also hired Black women as salespeople for her products. By employing and educating Black women on hair and skin care, Madam Walker created a generation of financially independent Black women at a time when they were actively kept from doing certain jobs, receiving services, and entering public spaces because of their appearance. Madam Walker knew that beauty trends could be a tool of white supremacy, and she did what she could to build her own tools to dismantle barriers that Black women faced in the US. Her tools were hair products and, later, makeup for those with black skin.

Before she started her company, Madam Walker's own hair had stopped growing and had fallen out. She had experienced the importance others placed on hair and skin color—and how one's social and professional life could be affected when her scalp was diseased and her head was balding. In advertisements, media, and everyday conversation, white people sent messages—such as comparing Black people's hair to sheep's wool—that were meant to dehumanize Black people and denigrate their appearance. White folks simply didn't see Black people as able to participate in the beauty industry because they didn't see them as people who could be beautiful.

Madam Walker worked to fight those messages. She believed that Black women could form their own styles and beauty culture. One Walker company advertisement had the phrase "GLORIFYING OUR WOMANHOOD" in large writing across the top and then went on to say "No greater force is working to glorify the womanhood of our Race than Madam C. J. Walker's Wonderful Hair and Skin Preparations."[4] Her advertisements and products specifically emphasized Black women's beauty and personhood, but her hair-care techniques sometimes drew criticisms from Black activists that she was aiming to conform to white women's beauty standards of long straight hair.

Although Madam Walker's techniques to promote hair growth did include a hot comb, which was used to straighten hair, she adamantly viewed herself as a "hair culturist" who grew hair, rather than someone who advertised that she could straighten Black women's hair. African American rights activist W. E. B. Du Bois's obituary of Madam Walker that said the hot comb was the least important part of her method and that the accusation that Black women were straightening their hair to imitate white women led Madam Walker to modify her method to create a more "natural-looking texture" for the Black women she served.[5] Her hair products emphasized regular shampooing and healing the scalp, creating the right environment for healthy hair to grow. Her hair products also prevented dandruff and other scalp diseases that were rampant in the early 1900s among Black and white women alike.

And it worked. Her hair-care system allowed thousands of Black women across the US to grow out and take care of their hair, which had ripple effects on the rest of their lives. One of Madam Walker's top agents wrote in a testimonial for a brochure, "You have opened up a trade for hundreds of our colored women to make an honest and profitable living . . . where they can make as much in one week as a month's salary would bring from any other position a colored woman can secure." A customer wrote, "It is a Godsend to unfortunate women who are walking in the rank and file that I had walked. It has helped us financially since 1910."[6]

After World War I ended, in 1918—and after Madam Walker's earnings increased about $100,000 over the previous year, emphasizing how large the market could be for selling grooming products to Black women—she expanded from hair care into cosmetics. Her line of facial products included cold cream, cleansing cream, witch hazel, and four shades of face powder.[7] At this time, Black women in the US were trying to find their place in a consumer culture that favored white skin and European beauty ideals. Black women with dark skin were generally either left out of mass-produced images in the beauty industry or they were included in dehumanizing ad campaigns depicting Black people as cartoonish brutes in need of grooming and refinement. In before and after pictures that depicted what women would look like when they used a certain product, caricatures of Black women were typically the before and light-skinned or white women the after, emphasizing that white skin was the beauty ideal women should aim for.

Starting a new trend, Madam Walker inserted herself into advertising images by using her own face. Using images of her own hair to prove the effects of her products showed that Black women could not only be customers but also could be a part of the images and advertisements that made up beauty culture. She wasn't just the before image for her products—she was the after as well, signaling that Black women could aspire to be beautiful too.[8] And by using her own story as a former laundress who created a successful cosmetics company, Madam Walker made other women believe they could aspire to higher-paid positions and gain more financial independence themselves, just as she did.[9] Instead of treating Black women as an afterthought, she centered Black women in a country that refused to do so.

———

Because lighter skin can be perceived as a visual indicator of a higher class, some people turn to products that claim to actually lighten skin. Many cultures around the world have their own skin-lightening concoctions and products. Before mass-marketed beauty products in the 1900s, women would create their own cosmetics or beauty remedies at home, including finding ways to bleach their skin. Peroxide and buttermilk were just two household products that could be used to lighten skin tone or get rid of freckles.[10] When manufacturers began producing cosmetics in the late 1800s and early 1900s during the emergence of the mass-market beauty industry in the US, skin lightening and bleaching creams were some of the few types of products companies made and advertised, knowing that there was a demand from both white women and women of color.

One such product, known as Wonderful Face Bleach, promised to lighten the skin of a Black or brown person by four or five shades or turn a multiracial person perfectly white.[11] One advertisement for this product called it a "Black skin remover"—not bothering to hide its harmful racist goal in softer language.[12] Some Black newspapers refused to run ads for hair straightening or skin-bleaching products like Wonderful Face Bleach because they didn't want to reinforce the message that Black people needed to "fix" their appearance. Civil rights leader Booker T. Washington was long opposed to cosmetics manufacturers, in part because he believed they pushed white beauty standards onto Black women.[13] It even took him a while to warm up to Madam Walker herself, though he eventually welcomed her into his social circles and conventions and organizations that promoted Black-owned businesses.

Madam Walker didn't sell bleaching creams at her company while she was alive. Just as with her hair products, she emphasized that Black women could be beautiful and take pride in their appearance without assimilating to white women's beauty standards. However, after her death in 1919, the Walker company did sell bleaching products, including a product called Tan-Off, which was used for "brightening" dark skin or for the "treatment of tan, freckle, skin-blotch and for clearing the complexion."[14] Although some Black women used bleaching creams and lightening powders in the 1920s and '30s, others spoke out against such products. Through newspaper editorials and conferences, business owners and activists worked to combat the idea that there was anything wrong with Black women's natural appearance.

In response to some of the criticism, many white-owned beauty firms rewrote their advertising copy to appear less explicitly racist the 1920s.[15] Instead of saying bleaching products would whiten skin, they claimed they could provide a bright complexion—like the

Walker company's Tan-Off product. "This use of the word *bright* had a double meaning: By smoothing rough or uneven skin, creams did brighten, in a sense, by improving the reflectivity of light, but among African Americans the term had a distinct connotation, that of light brown skin," wrote historian Kathy Peiss.[16] The word *bright*—and other advertising jargon—is coded language that can be used to subtly reinforce racist beauty ideals. The idea of bright skin doesn't exclusively indicate racism, of course, but that's part of what makes white supremacy so hard to spot and to stop. Creams that promote making dark skin white can be obviously called out as problematic; creams that promise to brighten complexions are not obviously—or even always—bad.

———

Outside of bleaching or brightening creams, Black women generally had to make their own products if they wanted cosmetics that catered to them. Before cosmetics could be mass-produced, many people used family recipes for skin care and cosmetics, like burned cork to darken lashes. In the early 1900s in the US, many women continued to use folk recipes, especially if they were poor or lived in rural areas. As cosmetics began to be produced on a mass-market scale, the makeup factories produced was generally for white women.

When Black folks like Anthony Overton and Madam Walker entered the beauty market and created skin-care and hair-care products, they typically had to do so by creating smaller companies than those that served white women. Beauty companies owned by Black people or that served Black women often had to sell products door-to-door or through mail-in orders because white-owned national magazines and large department stores wouldn't run ads for or stock their products.

In the early 1900s, when cosmetic powerhouses like Max Factor, Elizabeth Arden, and Helena Rubinstein started their companies in the US, they created makeup for white skin and aimed to sell

An 1896 painting of Cleopatra, the last pharaoh of Egypt, by Frederick Arthur Bridgman.

An eighteenth-century illustration of Empress Wu, the only woman emperor in ancient China.

The Darnley Portrait showed Queen Elizabeth I how she wanted to be seen.

Madam C. J. Walker, the first female self-made millionaire in America, circa 1914.

Sabella Nitti received a makeover during her 1923 murder trial.

Clara Bow, one of Hollywood's first sex symbols.

Marilyn Monroe's signature makeup look.

Josephine Baker used her beauty as a cover for her work as a spy.

Lena Horne had to navigate racism in Hollywood.

Elizabeth Taylor, made up for her role in *Cleopatra*, 1963.

Pan Am and other airlines required flight attendants to maintain a certain appearance.

David Bowie performs as Ziggy Stardust in 1973.

Marsha P. Johnson a few months before her death in 1992.

Yoshiko Shinohara, the founder and president of Tempstaff Co., 2008.

Tsuyoshi Kusanagi of the boy band SMAP.

James Charles became CoverGirl's first male spokesperson in 2016.

Rihanna attends a launch for Fenty Beauty in 2017.

Alexandria Ocasio-Cortez at her congressional swearing-in ceremony in 2019.

Micaela Iron Shell raising awareness of the Missing and Murdered Indigenous Women movement, 2019.

Kim Kardashian, 2011.

products to white customers. Arden especially prized being a part of the white upper-class society crowd, selling her products at high prices in high-end stores to get and maintain an exclusive rich white clientele. It took years for manufacturers like these to expand their shade range and to think of Black women as customers to court—if they ever came around.

But some US companies did aim to serve Black women right at the start of the modern beauty industry. Although he began by making baking powder, Overton saw that Black women didn't have makeup to match their skin tones, so he created a powder makeup, High-Brown Face Powder—one of the first specifically made for Black women. His Overton-Hygienic Manufacturing Company became successful, inspiring other people to make shades for Black women as well, including Madam Walker, Black opera singer Anita Patti Brown with her brand Patti's Beauty Emporium, and Hungarian American Morton Neumann with his company Valmor Products.[17] However, an influx of beauty products for Black women didn't necessarily pave the way for an acceptance of Black beauty in society.

In the years following the Civil War, Americans of all races struggled to define a new American culture after slavery. Black people were trying to find a place in the culture and the economy of the US as free people, but they found that society was unwelcoming. Along with discrimination that kept Black people from jobs, education, property ownership, voting, and more, one of the most popular forms of entertainment during this period was the minstrel show, which used makeup to satirize and demean the lives of Black people.

The minstrel show was a satirical variety show that often made fun of class, gender, and racial differences while generally reinforcing the status quo of patriarchy and white supremacy. Minstrel shows were largely defined by the blackface makeup that white actors wore to portray stereotypes of Black people. Blackface makeup was made of burnt champagne corks and water or sometimes petroleum jelly.[18] To perform certain roles, white actors would "black up" with this dark substance, leaving space around their mouths to give the impression of thicker lips and exaggerated African American features.

This makeup created an "other" so that white audiences could look at exaggerated differences between themselves and Black people, even when the jokes or songs weren't directly about race. Moreover, the makeup meant that all-white performance troops didn't have to hire Black actors to portray Black characters, further reinforcing the division. Blackface makeup became a costume that actors could inhabit and hide behind. It also indicated exaggeration and parody, with actors using the blackface makeup as an excuse to become a caricature instead of a well-rounded, fleshed-out character. The appearance of an actor in blackface signaled a joke to come—at the expense of Black people. Eventually, blackface makeup became a marker of some of the first purely American culture.[19]

These shows made fun of and appropriated Blackness and were created by white people, performed by white people, for audiences of white people. Minstrel shows' songs and dances became a foundation for the evolution of the entertainment business in the US—and so did the stereotypes the minstrel show promoted. In Hollywood, white writers, directors, and actors brought the stereotypes developed on the minstrel stage to the movie screen. In addition, the film industry greatly influenced the beauty industry. Both industries were built on upholding images that reinforced whiteness at the expense of Black people. Movies and movie stars also had a great effect on both the culture of the US and what makeup trends people took part in.

After the Civil War, minstrel shows in some cases became a showcase for Black performers, who sometimes adopted minstrel show tropes and subverted them. Hattie McDaniel was one Black actor who had performed in blackface before making a career in Hollywood. When she began acting in movies, McDaniel continued playing maids and mammies for years, using her performance to add depth and subvert expectations when she could, just as she had when she performed in minstrel shows. Eventually, McDaniel became the first Black female actor to be nominated for and win an Oscar for her portrayal of Mammy in *Gone with the Wind*. But these characters also tended to reinforce harmful ideas that Black women were happy to remain subservient to white people even after emancipation and that they were obedient and loyal to their white masters. These roles didn't use makeup to indicate glamour the way other movie star roles did because they were meant to portray plain, sexless characters. McDaniel attempted to add agency to her characters, but the stereotype of the Black maid remained.

For McDaniel, playing the mammy stereotype was the only way she could get roles in movies at all. She had to weigh playing stereotypes against not working as an actor, and acting made significantly more money than the domestic work she resorted to repeatedly throughout her life. She had been known to say, "I can be a maid for seven dollars a week, or I can play a maid for seven hundred dollars a week."[20] When McDaniel gave advice to up-and-coming Black actor Lena Horne, who was wondering how to navigate finding roles for Black actors in Hollywood, McDaniel told her to do what she had to do to keep working and feed her family.[21] During their careers, both McDaniel and Horne had to learn to navigate the systemic racism of Hollywood that promoted racist ideas based on blackface portrayals of minstrel show stereotypes. And both actors faced criticism from some Black activists for being a part of this system and thus promoting those limited characterizations of Black people in movies.

When Horne began her career in film in the late 1930s and early '40s, Hollywood was supposedly ready to try to create a new kind of Black movie star. Because of pushback from the NAACP and other activists complaining about Hollywood's portrayals of Black people, some studios decided to at least look like they wanted to make improvements.

Horne was the first Black performer to sign a full studio contract when she signed with MGM in 1942. The studio claimed that her roles wouldn't all be Black maids to white women.[22] Horne was the first Black woman in Hollywood to be promoted and marketed as glamorous. She drew interest from movie studios in part because she was beautiful in a way that resembled white beauty standards. She had light skin and a narrow frame and exuded an air of sophistication quite different from the image of Black womanhood the movies usually promoted. It looked like she could become a movie star with star power similar to a white leading lady—but it didn't quite turn out that way.

Because white Hollywood executives defined glamour based on white beauty standards and ignored or didn't see the glamorous Black women who existed off the movie screen, MGM struggled to imagine a role for Horne—a glamorous Black woman. At the time, such a character hadn't yet appeared in mainstream media and would have to be "invented" by white studio executives who wanted the role to be marketable to white audiences—and easy to cut from films if those audiences didn't want it. The studios' difficulty portraying a Black woman as glamorous was amplified by the studio's lack of makeup for darker skin. For help, MGM turned to Max Factor, the man whose makeup company produced and supplied makeup for the movies and who acted as makeup artist for many stars in Hollywood.

But the studio asked to make Horne's light skin appear darker.[23] After hiring Horne in part because her beauty could be read as white, the studio decided she needed to look darker to be read on screen as Black. Instead of allowing for the fact that Black people have different skin tones and using the makeup that best suited Horne's skin, MGM and Max Factor contributed to racist ideas of what Black people should look like and what should be represented on film. So the company created a new makeup called Light Egyptian especially for Horne.[24] But it was much too dark, and the results didn't look good on camera. The lack of vision and acceptance for her beauty, and the lack of makeup options that actually matched her skin tone, likely hampered her career in film, where makeup and hairstyling were understood to be a part of the image movie stars portrayed. Eventually, after spending time trying to find the best way to make up, light, and photograph Horne, the studio decided to light and photograph her in the same way as white actors—although their treatment of Horne showed they did not view her as beautiful in the same way.[25]

Later in Horne's career, after promoting her as a glamorous Black actor, the studio did not give her the lead part in 1951's *Show Boat*. The studio said that now Horne was too recognizably Black, and the part in the film was about a Black woman who could pass as white. The lead in *Show Boat* instead went to white actor Ava Gardner. To make Gardner's skin look darker, they used Max Factor's Light Egyptian makeup—the same makeup they made for Horne that was much too dark.[26] So, after declaring Horne as "too Black" for the role, the studio then used makeup on Gardner that made her skin look *darker* than Horne's skin. After Horne fit into the image the studio wanted her to portray, the studio later changed the rules, keeping her career from accelerating and promoting a white actor instead. But Horne couldn't move forward in the film business without the studio's support in the first place, putting her in an unwinnable situation. Eventually, it became too much. She stopped making movies by the mid-1950s, turning instead to performing in nightclubs and variety shows on television.

Today white makeup artists meant to help actors prepare for their roles often don't have products for darker skin in their kits or even know how to apply makeup to black or brown skin. For models and actors in the twenty-first century who are part of an industry that decides what's fashionable and would presumably have greater access to makeup, women of color's makeup needs are still often excluded from makeup artists' supply kits.

In March 2019, Black actors talked on social media about their experiences having their makeup and hair done on set, often by makeup artists and hairstylists who have little or no experience working with Black people. Using the hashtag #ActingWhileBlack, actors Yahya Abdul-Mateen, Yvette Nicole Brown, Gabrielle Union, and others discussed how they prepare for a set that may not be prepared to work with them. That may include going to a hairstylist before going to set, bringing personal wigs to set, or even getting their makeup done entirely before they show up to work. Makeup artists and hairstylists on film and TV sets often need to be part of a union to work on the set—but getting into the union is a difficult process and one that, like many of the projects they work on, favors whiteness and experience working with white skin and white people's hair. So makeup artists and hairstylists who focus on working with Black people may have more trouble getting into the union than those who focus on white people. The difficulties of navigating makeup for Black people in the film industry becomes a microcosm for how Black beauty is navigated in the rest of society.

———

These impossible standards aren't only in show business. All over the world, people believe that lighter skin indicates not just beauty but also wealth and privilege. And all over the world, makeup and beauty trends are used to reinforce the white supremacist idea that white skin is better. "The white face, purged of the exertions of labor, simultaneously asserted bourgeois refinement and racial privilege," Peiss wrote.[27] When European colonialism spread throughout the world, it brought with it the message that white skin is preferable.

The mass-market makeup brand CoverGirl, founded in 1961, played a role in promoting whiteness as an American ideal of beauty. The company used white models in its advertising, describing the look it wanted to promote with words like "American," "fresh," and "clean."[28] Amid the civil rights movement of the 1960s, some white-owned beauty companies in the US started to change how they created and promoted products for Black women, and some major firms like Revlon and Avon entered the "ethnic" cosmetics field in the 1970s. While beauty companies like Avon were expanding their shade ranges and actively seeking women of color as customers—and understanding that women of color also wanted to be viewed as American—CoverGirl offered only seven shades of foundation for many years, with most of those shades meant for white women and only a few to match women of color.[29] CoverGirl hired its first Black model to be a face of the brand in 1992 when it signed a contract with Lana Ogilvie. Over the next decades, along with the increase in shades from other mass-market brands, CoverGirl expanded its shade range to twenty-one for certain products. In 2018—after Rihanna's Fenty line entered the market in 2017 with forty shades—Cover Girl finally expanded its shade range for certain foundations to forty colors.[30]

When pop star Rihanna started Fenty, she made sure to include many shades that are dark, along with shades that are extremely light, to give people the option to match their skin tones no matter what color their skin is. Although Fenty started with forty foundation shades, it has since expanded further to fifty in 2019. After its first month, Fenty recorded $72 million in earned media value, which attempts to measure exposure to the brand that doesn't come from paid advertising—so things like social media and word of mouth.[31] No matter how you measure it, it's clear that Fenty has influenced the beauty industry. Because of Rihanna's success, more makeup companies started expanding their shade range—just as more companies created makeup for Black women following the success of Anthony Overton.

But the beauty industry as a whole still does not prioritize dark skin. Bleaching products remain popular in many countries worldwide, continuing to reinforce whiteness as a beauty ideal. Although many regions and cultures created their own types of bleaching products to treat discoloration in skin or to make skin appear smoother and brighter before European imperialism, the tendency to value lighter skin certainly grew stronger and spread further thanks to colonialism. A report from Grand View Research says the global market for skin-lightening products was valued at $8.3 billion in 2018 and will rise to $13.7 billion by 2025. Asia-Pacific led the market in 2018 at 54.3 percent of global revenue and is expected to see the most growth over the period.[32]

A 2017 article in *Marie Claire* titled "Why Black Women in a Predominately Black Culture Are Still Bleaching Their Skin" explores the use of bleaching creams in Jamaica. Rebekah Kebede wrote that, historically, Jamaicans with lighter brown skin were the product of relationships between Black Jamaicans and white enslavers or colonial rulers.[33] Because of that, even today in Jamaica, lighter skin is still often believed to be an indicator of a social class that has greater privilege and access to resources. Jody Cooper, a Jamaican woman interviewed in the article, said she bleached her skin in part to try to get more work as a hairstylist. Image is a big part of her job, so she felt more people would trust her to do their hair if she had the lighter skin that society around her deemed preferable.

In many places, fitting into white and Eurocentric beauty standards can often be part of getting and keeping public-facing or service jobs and receiving other social benefits based on appearance. In India in 2019, photographs of Miss India contestants sparked criticism that all the women had a similar light skin tone. Miss India is a huge cultural event where the women participating are primed for a global stage—and on that stage, judges prioritize European beauty standards of fairer skin.[34] An image of these women all next to each other emphasized their similar hair and skin colors and seems to have touched on something especially sensitive for India, which has a history with the caste system, where people in a lower caste were associated with having darker skin. Once again, just like in Jamaica and the US, lighter skin is associated with more wealth, more privilege, and a higher class.

Use of bleaching products and the idea that lighter skin is indicative of beauty or wealth doesn't just affect women—men use bleaching creams, and children are also affected by colorism, or discrimination or prejudice against those with darker skin tones, even among people of the same racial group. Television personality and *Queer Eye* host Tan France, whose parents are Pakistani, wrote in his 2019 memoir *Naturally Tan* that he took skin-bleaching products from his cousin to use when he was just ten years old. He wrote that, even at that young age, he desperately wanted to have white skin because he believed it would make him more attractive and happier in life.[35] While growing up in the UK, France had seen people in his South Asian community ask if newborn babies were fair skinned, emphasizing their belief that light skin was preferable.

These bleaching products can cause physical harm, along with emotional harm. Black pharmacist Mrs. J. H. P. Coleman noted at a National Negro Business League conference in 1912 that the person promoting Wonderful Face Bleach wore gloves, suggesting that gloves wouldn't be necessary if it were safe to use on Black people's skin.[36] There were also multiple reports of Wonderful Face Bleach causing blindness, even though ads for the product claimed it was safe to use on eyelids. Wonderful Face Bleach is no longer made, but other bleaching products that exist today can still cause harm to those who use them. Ingredients in some bleaching products include mercury and hydroquinone, which can poison the user, leading to skin damage and kidney and liver issues, among other side effects.[37] Some bleaching products and ingredients are banned in certain places, but even where they are illegal, a black market can likely provide illicit skin bleaching products for customers who want them. Though no studies have been specifically conducted to find out for sure, it's possible that in some areas, it may be easier for someone to buy illegal bleaching products than it is to find mass-produced makeup that matches darker skin.

Some women have faced difficulties finding the right shade of makeup for their skin, having to drive many miles to find a store that carries the correct shade or needing to spend more money on expensive brands. Andrea Arterbery wrote in 2015 in *Cosmopolitan* of her own experience shopping at Walmart to replace a makeup item that broke: "While there were dozens of shades, not one suited my olive undertones. I knew from years of trial and error that, once applied, those pale shades would give me that 'trashy ashy' look. My frustration grew as I searched for darker colors that I could mix with a lighter shade."[38]

Some women have even faced open hostility while shopping. In 2017, Tansy Breshears wrote on Racked about her experience working as a manager at a kind of dollar store, where she had asked those higher up in her company about stocking makeup for women of color. Management replied that they didn't carry darker shades of makeup because they expected those products to get shoplifted.[39] Their response implied that women with dark skin would steal products meant for them and that lighter-skinned women wouldn't. The store dealt with this by excluding customers with darker skin.

Even if high-end makeup companies like Fenty provide a variety of shades, there is still a need for affordable drugstore products to include darker shades of makeup. Not having inexpensive makeup available in easily accessible stores adds a tax of time and money for Black and brown women to find makeup that works for them.

It was a good business decision for Rihanna to include such a variety of shades when she created Fenty, but she's clear that she was also motivated by a desire to illuminate the beauty of Black skin. What people in power call beautiful reflects what they deem valuable, and that in turn determines who gets certain resources, including access to certain jobs, the ability to shop without harassment in stores, access to medical care, and support in justice systems, among other privileges that make life easier and safer. Although all women face pressure to meet beauty standards, women of color have to work much harder to meet the standards of a beauty industry born from white supremacy. This is as true for women shopping in drugstores as it is for movie stars—a white supremacist society and the image it promotes can hurt everyone.

POW(D)ERFUL

In the year 710 AD in China, a coup and then a countercoup occurred in fairly quick succession, within just a few weeks. In the second coup, Princess Anle, the youngest daughter of Empress Wei and Emperor Zhongzong, was beheaded. The legends and stories surrounding her death claim that as she prepared to leave the palace when violence broke out, conspirators found her in front of her mirror because she took too long putting on her makeup.[1]

After her death, Chinese histories described Anle as vain, caring more about her image in a mirror than her own life. Descriptions of vanity become a common refrain after a powerful woman loses power. A poem written six hundred years after she died by Yang Weizhen, translated by scholar Rebecca Doran, describes Anle as unaware of the violence coming for her as she stands before the mirror: "As the thousand cavalry of the imperial guard give out their battle cry, she paints her eyebrows, paints her eyebrows before the break of dawn."[2]

There is no way to know if Anle was actually putting on makeup when she was killed. Stories about women in power tend to morph into legends that emphasize frivolity and vanity. But she likely knew that her status came in part from her image. And she likely knew that without her appearance that indicated her status, her life outside the palace had fewer options or was nonexistent. Some men who write histories of powerful women portray vanity as shallow, evil, and something to avoid—a warning for women who may try to manipulate the system by using their appearance to gain influence. But for a princess whose value and privilege in part depended on her looks and the markers of status they portrayed, it may have made sense to spend time cultivating and protecting her appearance, even at risk of her life.

For people who hold power all over the world, it is important to project strength. This is especially true for sovereign leaders because the government largely depends on one person. Leaders of all genders have historically pursued a youthful appearance to demonstrate that their government is stable and enduring. But when male leaders build muscle, groom their hair, or wear refined clothing to project youth, strength, and stability, they are viewed as capable and charismatic. For women in cultures that don't view them as capable of leading their own households, much less a nation, their projection of stability and strength takes on even greater importance but is recast as vanity. In a world where women have had to fight for property and power, which is not always legally granted even today, some women reach for tools to take more control of their lives and their image— which often end up being the same thing.

———

There's a reason that women who managed to gain power throughout history were often legendary beauties: they had to be beautiful to gain status, and once they were in power, their looks and choices helped set the fashion trends and beauty conventions they were then measured against. Egypt's Cleopatra was another ruler who became known for her beauty, as was the Mughal Empire's Nur Jahan. In the 1500s in England, Queen Elizabeth I portrayed a white face and rosy cheeks to indicate perfect, virginal femininity and inspired women at court to also sport white faces with pink cheeks and red hair. This pattern is also evident in the modern world in the way both world leaders and celebrities gain status and power. US celebrity Kim Kardashian gained influence in part because of how her looks demonstrated an aspirational lifestyle. As a way to reinforce her status, she set makeup trends that placed herself as the top example of how those trends should look.

Anle was following the road map to gain power that her grandmother, Empress Wu, had laid out before her and that many other women have followed since: use makeup to create a self-image that emphasizes wealth and youth. Wu used her image as a pretty teenage girl to first put herself in the position to be near the politically powerful as a concubine to the emperor. Wu was not from a notable or high-class family in China's history—she was the daughter of a merchant who became a government official in the Tang dynasty. After her father died, her family sent her to the palace of the Emperor Taizong, possibly as a way for her mother to make sure her daughter was cared for. In part because of her beauty even as a girl, she became a fifth-ranked concubine for the emperor. The empress was the main wife and the mother of the emperor's legitimate heirs, and below the empress were eight levels of concubines. Each level of concubine closer to the emperor gained glamour and prestige, using more elaborate makeup and hairstyles to indicate their status. Over decades, Wu cultivated her image by wearing lavish cosmetics to indicate her rising status and increase her visibility in public. She slowly transitioned out of the conventions in her culture for a woman, which emphasized domesticity and patriarchal rule. By breaking conventions and garnering political power, Wu become the only female emperor in China to rule under her own name.

Wu was known to have been particularly gifted with makeup.[3] Society women in China in the Tang dynasty like Wu used white lead for face paint and cinnabar or vermilion to make rouge for their cheeks and lips. They would also pluck out or shave their eyebrows and draw on patches of a green shadow high on the forehead, called moth eyebrows. In the early seventh century, this style, which resembled the wings of the insect, was so popular that officials supplied a daily ration of twenty-seven quarts of pigment to the emperor's concubines.[4] Later, in the eighth and ninth centuries, styles of eyebrows included a V shape or three or four red or purple lines above and below the eye.[5] For good luck, women in the Tang dynasty may have added litharge—a lead oxide—to create a yellow tint to their foreheads and brow areas.[6]

There are no paintings or images of Wu from her own time, but paintings of her from later periods illustrate her with thin painted eyebrows, with three lines painted below her eyes and three dots in the center of her forehead. What remains from her time are stories of the glamorous version of herself she created. Her natural beauty may have been striking, but it was her understanding of her cultural context that allowed her to manipulate others' perceptions of her using a studied combination of makeup and charisma.[7] She used elaborate makeup to maintain an image of strength, youth, and beauty, hiding wrinkles and flaws in her skin and emphasizing her status as emperor as she gained power in her old age.[8] And when she was younger, Wu and other concubines used their looks to try to attract attention from the emperor—the man who largely controlled their lives. Access to the emperor meant a possible promotion to a higher level of concubine, greater material goods, and possibly bearing a child for the emperor, raising the status of the concubine even higher.

Wu gained status by using her looks to gain attention from powerful people. When Taizong became ill, Wu attended to him, and her beauty drew the attention of Taizong's son Gaozong, who was spending time with his dying father. Around this time, Wu and Gaozong began a relationship. Folklore tells a story of the first time she and Gaozong were intimate by describing Gaozong leaving the room to go to the bathroom and coming back to find Wu kneeling on the floor and offering a bowl of water to wash his hands. In the story, he splashes the water on her face and says that the water has ruined her powder. When she flirted back, their relationship began.[9]

That this legend references her face powder indicates the kind of beauty Wu embodied. Although Wu may have been in simpler clothing and makeup while acting as a nurse or maid for Taizong during his illness, the mention of face powder is still a reference to that kind of made-up beauty that belonged to a higher class of woman in the palace.

In certain past dynasties, when an emperor died, his concubines were killed. When Taizong died, the concubines who had children with him were sent to a palace for retirement. The others, however, would have been sent to a nunnery for the rest of their lives. Instead of elaborate hairstyles that they wore in court, the women in the nunnery would be expected to shave their heads—indicating an abandonment of the stylings of the palace. For Wu, a young woman at the time, the life she knew came to an end.

Her relationship with Gaozong changed her fate, though it didn't come without some risk. Because Wu had been a concubine of Gaozong's father, some viewed her relationship with Gaozong as inappropriate, similar to incest. But Gaozong eventually brought her back to the palace, and Wu became one of his second-level concubines. Wu wasn't expected to rise any higher—partly because she didn't come from an aristocratic family. But Wu gained favor with certain people in court and placed herself in a position for Gaozong to prefer her over his wife, the Empress Wang.[10] After several plots and scandals that hurt Wang's image, Gaozong asked his ministers to remove Wang as empress and install Wu.

Removing an empress was not a simple thing for Gaozong to do. The court didn't easily approve it, and some ministers even warned him that Wu's beauty alone was not enough of a qualification for her to become an empress.[11] These warnings to Gaozong made it clear that the men in court saw beauty as a thing to be feared for its seductive qualities that could distract men to ruin, and that they viewed women as either sexual or good political allies, but not both. Wu's challenge was to combine the seductive image of beauty that placed her near power with the power she wanted to wield.

Before Wu was enthroned as empress in 655, Gaozong imprisoned his former empress, Wang, along with another concubine, based on charges (likely falsified) that they had conspired together to poison him. In the room where they were held, the women were denied the bath attendants, luxurious clothing, and other markers of status or wealth.[12] Stripped of her title and demoted to a commoner, without the clothing and makeup that marked her as a valued member of the royal family, Wang was indistinguishable from the common people.

Using clothing and cosmetics to indicate status was ingrained in the Tang dynasty culture, and Wang wasn't the only woman who would have been punished in part by taking away tools to control their appearance. Wives of noblemen would punish enslaved people or concubines by branding their faces—thus permanently detracting from their beauty. Tang women would paint beauty marks on their face with red, yellow, black, or other pigments, and sometimes they made beauty marks into the shapes of moons, birds, insects, or flowers.[13] These marks could cover blemishes or scars—thus hiding the ones branded onto their faces and erasing a physical mark that indicated their lower status. Beauty marks came back into style around the year 700 after a woman who had previously been enslaved became a secretary to Wu and reintroduced the marks to noble society. Because women in higher classes also wore beauty marks, they became a way for a woman to use makeup to traverse class.

The color of clothing in the Tang dynasty also portrayed what status men and women held, with officials of certain levels wearing robes of certain colors and wives wearing the same color as their husbands.[14] Because these rules were tied to men who occupied positions in the government, only men could be dismissed from office or punished if they violated dress codes. Women who broke the rules were not in danger of losing their status; rather, they could gain prestige by using makeup and clothing to appear to be in a higher social class. This stoked sexist views that women were untrustworthy social climbers, when really they were using the tools accessible to them, like robes or beauty marks, to gain social benefits.[15] A woman's status was tied to the men in her family, but sartorial choices were under an individual's control, so using those tools could be the only way some women had access to the benefits that a higher class provided. As Wu gained status in the palace and increased her participation in government affairs, certain male officials believed her social climbing made her untrustworthy when she tried to gain power for herself. This belief that women are untrustworthy, vain, and obsessed with status persists today, and this myth continues to bind a woman's worth to her appearance.

Even after Wu gained power, she couldn't be seen as having official forms of power. Gaozong had experienced bouts of sickness throughout his life, and in 660, he experienced what was likely a stroke. He turned to Wu for help, and for many years, she ruled with Gaozong. Wu would often sit behind a curtain during meetings with Gaozong, and the two would deliberate administrative decisions. This curtain indicates that even though she was an active participant, she still couldn't act as the face of the government.

One way she increased her visibility in government was to instigate and participate in a rare powerful Chinese religious ceremony known as Feng Shan in 666, which was meant to indicate the peak of an emperor's reign. Wu pushed for the ceremony to happen, then pushed for a role in it for herself, insisting that women were necessary for the correct order of the world. In her culture and in the dominant religion of Confucianism, there was a perception that women belonged to the private domestic sphere and men to the visible public sphere.[16] Wu also made sure that she herself was visible. When Wu traveled with her and Gaozong's court in ceremonies and in processions, she wore the extravagant clothing and makeup of an empress, which may have helped onlookers see her from afar. From a distance, her makeup would have shown smooth, flawless skin that appeared youthful and beautiful even as she grew older.

After Gaozong died in 683, Wu held on to power as her son became emperor. Zhongzong's first reign lasted about two months before Wu exiled him for being too deferential to his wife and installed her youngest son as emperor, known as Emperor Ruizong. Throughout these changes, Wu made administrative and political decisions, essentially acting as the leader of the government. In 690, Ruizong yielded his power to Wu officially, and she took power under her own name, instead of the name of her husband or son, to establish the Zhou Dynasty. Women who transgress conventions of femininity by behaving in a way that their community views as masculine—like starting a new dynasty—often face backlash for those actions. Wu's clothing and makeup created a shield of femininity that covered her as she exercised her own agency in sometimes violent ways.

Wu's reign came to an end after conspirators orchestrated the coup that installed her exiled son Zhongzong again as emperor in 705. After the coup, Wu was sent to a palace outside of the imperial city and essentially placed under house arrest. No longer in power, Wu stopped taking care of her appearance, brushing her hair, or washing her face.[17] The condition of her hair and makeup mirrored her rise and fall from power. No longer an emperor, Wu didn't need to maintain her image because she had already lost the status it portrayed.

In England in the 1500s, another ruler created a striking image of her own when she came into power. In her most famous portrait, a crown of pearls weaves across the top of Queen Elizabeth I's orangey-red curls. A white ruffle around her neck frames her ghostly face and serious, deep brown, round eyes. Her white forehead slopes high on the top of her head to meet a receded hairline, as was fashionable at the time of her reign. Her oval face comes to a soft point in her small chin under red lips. Her pearlescent white skin is free of any wrinkles or blemishes, even though she was around forty years old at the time she sat for this painting. Her eyebrows are almost nonexistent in the faded image—which was once vibrant and portrayed much rosier skin. One can still see the faint red of her cheeks that must have been bright in the 1570s, when an artist whose name is unknown made this painting.

This portrait, known as the Darnley Portrait, is important not just because it survived her long reign, but also because it was used as a model painting for other artists to copy to make images of the queen. For many in her realm and throughout Europe, these portraits would be the only way to see England's ruler, so Elizabeth maintained strict control around her image to reinforce the idea of a powerful—beautiful—virgin queen.

As Elizabeth aged, she became more sensitive about wrinkles and sagging skin, and she felt that any clue that England's sovereign was aging and wouldn't live forever had no place in her palace. In 1596, when she was in her early sixties, Elizabeth even ordered paintings that depicted her as frail or ill to be destroyed.[18] That the Darnley portrait survived seems to indicate that it depicted Elizabeth as she wanted to be seen.

She never married and had no children, so there was no one to automatically succeed her as king or queen. Elizabeth felt that with the question of who would succeed her unresolved, she couldn't risk allowing her subjects to see any evidence of her advancing age. "Painters throughout history have flattered and idealised royalty, but in her case this was a deception that was deliberately maintained over a period of forty-five years," wrote historian Alison Weir.[19]

Elizabeth had reason to be wary of looking weak. Her path to the throne was unusual, and her claim to sovereignty was tenuous. Her mother was Anne Boleyn, the second of the six wives of King Henry VIII—and the first he ordered to die. Henry's son Edward from a subsequent marriage became the first in line to rule after Henry mainly because he was a man—even though he was nine years old when Henry died. He ruled until he was fifteen, when he named Lady Jane Grey as his successor. She was deposed before she was coronated, then the throne went to Elizabeth's sister Queen Mary, then, finally, to Elizabeth, when she was twenty-five years old. After so much speculation and so many beheadings and jailings (including a period Elizabeth herself spent in the Tower of London on Mary's orders), Elizabeth likely wanted to appear in control at all times. So she worked hard at looking the part.

A perfect vision of femininity in England at this time included white, porcelain skin; a high forehead, often achieved by plucking hairs from the hairline; and thin, plucked eyebrows. To get a pale complexion, wealthy women in England in this period would often use ceruse—a powder made of white lead mixed with vinegar—and other skin-lightening concoctions. Venetian ceruse was named for Venice, the pinnacle of European beauty at that time—and possibly one of the earliest instances of beauty branding.[20] Venetian ceruse was branded as the most exclusive, most expensive, and highest quality ceruse. Unfortunately, that meant it also had the highest concentration of lead—a poisonous ingredient that over time would damage skin by making it discolored and withered, cause hair to fall out, and even damage teeth and organs, like the lungs. In fact, the high hairline that was popular in the sixteenth century may have been a result of women's hair falling out from the chemicals, like lead, mercury, and arsenic, they were exposed to in cosmetics.

To lighten her complexion, Elizabeth used a lotion made from a combination of egg whites, powdered eggshell, alum, borax, poppy seeds, and mill water.[21] The egg whites in the makeup were to smooth scars from smallpox, which she had at twenty-nine. The mixture also reflected light, giving the skin a white, almost ghostly glow in the candlelight used as lighting at that time. She also used Venetian ceruse on and off throughout her life, especially for her smallpox scars.[22] Eventually, the poisonous ceruse would eat away at the skin to create more sores and scars, which would require more makeup to cover up those marks, thus beginning a cruel cycle of makeup application and skin damage.

The people of England would take their style cues from the queen, leading to legions of women using poisonous cosmetics to attempt to match her appearance. Women in Elizabeth's time would not only copy her pale white skin; they also dyed their hair or wore wigs to match the queen's red hair, which de facto became the trendy hair color during Elizabeth's reign. But dying hair during this time in England was almost as poisonous as painting your face with lead. To dye their hair red, women would use lye, rock alum, and saltpeter, all of which were toxic.[23] To dye their wigs, women would use a mixture of sulfur and safflower petals, which led to nosebleeds, headaches, and nausea.

The dangers of some of these materials didn't become fully known until hundreds of years later, but women still experienced the effects, whether they knew the scientific reasons for them or not. And because the health of women has been historically undervalued, there's no certainty that steps would have been taken to protect women from the effects of these ingredients even if they were recognized. Safety regulations for cosmetics wouldn't be created until after the industrial revolution, when makeup was made on a mass scale by machinery for the first time.[24]

Women who used these poisonous cosmetics decided any pain or discomfort was worth it for the benefits it gave them. Looking a certain way helped women gain favor with those at court, receive material wealth, or marry into a higher class; ignoring social customs like using certain makeup could lead to being ostracized and falling out of favor. The status and power that makeup helped create for these women provided enough social and material comfort to outweigh any physical discomfort. This is true for modern women who undergo chemical peels, waxing, or myriad other beauty procedures and products that can cause pain.

Elizabeth also painted her lips and cheeks red using vermilion, which was made of powdered cinnabar containing mercury. Mercury is easily absorbed in the skin and could lead to bad breath, loss of teeth, and swollen lips. Eventually, mercury could cause mental deterioration, paranoia, depression, and wild mood swings—all of which the queen suffered as she aged. On top of lead and mercury, some women applied face powder containing arsenic, which did make skin pale but could also cause scaly skin, headaches, confusion, cancer, and more.

A youthful white face promoted Elizabeth's image as a virgin—and in sixteenth-century England, this was important. Elizabeth was a single woman in one of the most powerful positions in the world. Government officials in patriarchal England generally didn't want a woman ruler in the first place, much less a woman that didn't have a man bound to her by matrimony to guide and control her. Her advisors also claimed they were concerned about stability for the country if there were no set plan for succession, so they encouraged her to consider marriage and having children. In their view, the easiest way to secure a spot on the throne after Elizabeth was for her to give birth to an heir—but women died in childbirth frequently at this time, so having children would have been a big risk to her life.

Elizabeth also had seen serious downsides to marriage. Her father famously married six times, and he separated from the Roman Catholic Church to create the Church of England when the pope wouldn't allow him to divorce his first wife. He executed his second wife, Elizabeth's mother. So instead of getting married herself, Elizabeth used her image to help create a myth of a queen who was beautiful enough to attract and entertain marriage proposals—which depended on her ensured virginity—all while ending the relationship before the marriage actually happened.

As a queen, Elizabeth knew she had more power as a single woman. If she were to get married, she would have to submit to her husband, according to the predominant religious and cultural beliefs in England at the time. Instead of being in control of her reign, she'd have to share it with a man and possibly lose control completely. To look like she wanted to get married, Elizabeth maintained relationships with eligible bachelors throughout Europe. She'd begin marriage negotiations—which were extensive and could include things like what religions she'd enforce in England or what wars she'd allow her navy to be a part of—and then she'd renege at the last minute. Often she'd make up a reason why this particular marriage could never work, all while acting like she was still pining away for the man in question. Pining may not seem very regal for a queen, but for a rosy-cheeked young virgin, it was expected. In this way, Elizabeth used every tool she had to support the idea of marriage while maintaining the image of her sexual purity, all toward the goal of holding onto her power. Empress Wu used her image in the same way—promoting an ideal of femininity that was often in contrast with how her actions could have been perceived.

Elizabeth's beauty and power were so entwined that years after she died, people critiqued the monarchy by criticizing her looks. In the late nineteenth century, writers and painters began to depict Elizabeth as a vain spinster, ridiculously trying to hold on to her youth by using cosmetics and wigs.[25] To chip away at Elizabeth's power, these men claimed she didn't fit into the image that she was trying to present.

Men have often come out against cosmetics, even during Elizabeth's rule, for a variety of reasons: that it goes against God's will, that it's trickery to use materials to change your looks, or that it's vain and selfish to care about your looks at all. Meanwhile, beauty conventions remain difficult to meet, and women are punished for not fitting into them, as well as for trying too hard to fit into them. When men later made Elizabeth look like a fool—literally, for they often drew her looking clown-like in exaggerated makeup—they were using an effective strategy of belittling a woman by equating her appearance with her worth and portraying her as foolish, silly, ugly, exaggerated, vain, and worthless. This works for the same reason it worked to help Elizabeth maintain her power: people in the dominant class tend to wear certain styles to differentiate and reinforce their status. By claiming Elizabeth didn't fit into that image, people may have started to doubt if she belonged.

Makeup remains a specifically gendered tool to help women navigate social standings, and balancing acceptable femininity and exercising power is difficult to do. In addition, conforming to certain styles that reinforce these barriers has its own cost. After knowing all the ways Elizabeth compromised and manipulated her image to hold onto power that men were granted without question, the Darnley Portrait becomes more sinister. Instead of a powerful woman in control of a kingdom, it depicts a woman trapped in the same conventions as her subjects. Her face is smooth because she couldn't afford to show her wrinkles. Her skin is white because she used poison to make herself look pure. Her white mask of youth becomes a death mask; her radiance becomes toxic. For all the ways Elizabeth and other women gained power in part because of their beauty, they still couldn't escape the trap of being beautiful.

———

Keeping up with conventions has always had dangerous consequences—especially for those who can't fit into them. Standards of beauty change depending on the culture and the time period, but they tend to be based on and set by the group of people in power. This leaves the poor and underrepresented, who face graver consequences for not fitting in, out of the beauty ideal.

There were Black men and women at the royal courts of Henry VII, Henry VIII, Elizabeth I, and James I, and Black men and women lived freely and participated in society in both the cities and countryside of Tudor England.[26] There is not much information on whether Black women participated in cosmetics trends of wealthy white women, like ceruse makeup, but there are clues as to how ideas of beauty changed over this time in England to discriminate against those with darker skin. As England began to participate in the slave trade in the late 1500s, racist attitudes developed as a way to justify enslaving people with dark skin, and beauty ideals that emphasized whiteness grew more apparent at this time.

Court masques were plays performed in court that glorified the monarchy. In 1605, *The Masque of Blackness*, written by English playwright Ben Jonson at the request of Queen Anne of Denmark, told the story of Ethiopian nymphs who were brought to England. White women at the court, including Anne, used blackface makeup on their skin to act in the play and tell the story of nymphs who become worried their dark skin was no longer beautiful. The nymphs were sent away from court so their skin could be turned from black to white. In a sequel, *The Masque of Beauty*, the nymphs, now white, were brought back to England having been "fixed."[27] These plays lay bare racist beliefs that white skin is superior. The white monarchy and court used these plays to make a statement about what was beautiful—one that kept Black women from being considered beautiful or powerful, as whiteness was clearly required to be either.

Because makeup is malleable and affordable, and because it can be washed off at the end of the day, it's a much more accessible tool to change social status than generational wealth or inheriting a title—which women throughout history were often kept from because of patriarchal laws preventing them from inheriting or holding onto property and wealth. Makeup can also transform physical features that may not align with the values of the dominant culture into features that fit into the zeitgeist, the way a beauty mark can cover up a scar. That meant that any white woman with the means to purchase or make cosmetics and a good sense for fashion trends could exploit this knowledge to gain a connection with the upper class.

In the mid-1700s, two sisters used their beauty to marry into a higher class. Around 1740, Elizabeth and Maria Gunning started getting noticed for their beauty. In 1748, they were invited to a ball at Dublin Castle, but since they didn't have gowns to wear, they borrowed costumes from the local theater to literally play the part of wealthier women.[28] Women all the time dressed the part they needed to play in society. When going to a party, women would wear makeup to emulate those in higher classes or to indicate an understanding of the formality and traditions of the event—just as women continue to do today. Demonstrating that understanding of rituals—by wearing a certain type of dress to a ball, or wearing heavier makeup in the evening than in the daytime—is itself a class marker.

A local earl gave Elizabeth and Maria's mother money to help them go to London, where the girls gained fame and social clout because of their beauty. Because of this social capital, the two sisters were able to marry into higher classes: Elizabeth married the Duke of Hamilton and Maria the Earl of Coventry.

Maria's husband apparently didn't like her to use cosmetics—even though he married her in large part because of the conventional beauty they helped her to achieve. At one point during a dinner, people say the earl chased her around a dining room as he tried to wipe the makeup from her face. But Maria defied him and continued to wear her makeup, demonstrating that for her, makeup was more than a tool for climbing the social ladder; it was a rare opportunity for personal agency and self-expression.

Like Queen Elizabeth, Maria used ceruse, and the lead in the makeup seeped into her skin. Maria died in 1760 when she was just twenty-seven, likely from lead poisoning as a result of the cosmetics she wore. At her funeral, thousands of people joined the procession. That so many people wanted to see her in death, and possibly emulated her in life, is a testament to the image she created and the power and status that it brought her.

The Gunning sisters were influencers before the internet, using their beauty to gain status and power that they were previously locked out of. In the twenty-first century, images can travel faster around the world, and beauty remains a tool to gain status and power. Celebrity Kim Kardashian is an excellent modern example of how this can work.

Kardashian started her career in reality TV by making appearances on *The Simple Life*, airing from 2003 to 2007, as a friend to Paris Hilton, who was one of the stars of the show. The following year, with the help of her family's connections and her growing publicity—resulting in part from a sex tape of her leaked without her permission—she became the star of her own reality show. In *Keeping Up with the Kardashians*, she used her beauty to help portray an affluent, aspirational lifestyle. Through her show, modeling, and acting, Kardashian gained media attention. Then when she had an audience, she used endorsements, beauty products, and social media to increase both her reach and net worth by selling images of herself on TV and in magazines and then selling the makeup products she used. Instead of using her beauty to marry into wealth, like the Gunning sisters, she used her looks to make her own money.

Modern women who have the ability to gain financial independence don't need to rely on attracting a wealthy husband to reach a higher class. For some women, using makeup can be a way to make money—by selling it, becoming a makeup artist, or modeling. Makeup can also be a way to simply gain attention or show off the appearance of wealth. Sharing makeup tips or perfecting certain makeup trends, for example, is also a form of social capital. When a woman has control over her life and finances, she also has control over the way she looks, the money she makes and spends, and the makeup she uses. Instead of depending on men in her life to attain the rewards for her beauty, she reaps them for herself.

Kardashian used a method of makeup application called contouring, often used in theater, to shade and lighten the skin to emphasize certain features. Like chiaroscuro in art, this play of light and shadow helps sculpt the face using makeup instead of a scalpel. In theater, it can help the audience see actors' emotions when the stage is far away. Kardashian's makeup helped highlight certain features on her face—she used contouring to make her cheekbones and jawline look sharper, her forehead appear smaller, and her nose seem thinner and shorter. She uses concealer to make her under-eye area appear bright, getting rid of any dark circles and helping to lighten and raise the cheekbone. She also uses this shading to make her lips appear fuller and thicker.

The face she has created spawned a lucrative business to help others get her look, placing Kardashian at the peak. Jia Tolentino wrote for the *New Yorker* about the ubiquitous beauty trends in the 2010s that are in part based on the look Kardashian made popular. She quoted plastic surgeon Jason Diamond: "I'd say that thirty per cent of people come in bringing a photo of Kim, or someone like Kim—there's a handful of people, but she's at the very top of the list, and understandably so." Kardashian capitalized on already existing beauty standards and repackaged them as something attainable for a regular person—if only they used contour makeup or went to the plastic surgeon too.

Like Queen Elizabeth, Kardashian uses more makeup more often than the average woman likely would. In an event she did with makeup artist Mario Dedivanovic, who has worked with Kardashian for more than a decade, the pair demonstrated a fifty-step makeup routine, with custom products and products that weren't yet available to the general public. "This routine is impossible to reproduce," wrote Arabelle Sicardi for Racked in 2015.[29] Kardashian's custom colors and elaborate routine reinforce her superiority when it comes to makeup. People can try to look like her, but they'll never be able to get it exactly right because they don't have the resources and access she has.

Kardashian's makeup also emphasizes features associated with Black women, like thick lips. "The Kardashians have perfected their not-too-dark-but-not-too-light skin tone, their plump lips, and their rounded butts—they go to immense efforts to obtain black features," wrote Lindsay Peoples for The Cut in 2015.[30] In a society like the US that is built on white supremacy, Kardashian's whiteness gives her protection and privilege that Black women with the same features don't receive. Teryn Payne wrote for *Glamour* in 2018 that casting agents discriminate against Black models, with agents claiming that "having full lips and noses just doesn't work." Meanwhile, Kardashian makes millions of dollars promoting her own full lips, which she gets with the help of cosmetics.

Like makeup that emphasizes certain facial features, privilege highlights what the dominant culture deems important or preferable. When stylish makeup is combined with proximity to a higher class, wealth, and other privileges like whiteness, being cisgender, or being able-bodied, it creates an image of power that a person can leverage to create even more power. Often, a woman can't be powerful without certain markers that indicate beauty, either because she's perfecting the cosmetic and appearance trends that are already in place in her society, or because once she gains power, her proximity to power in effect sets the trends that define beauty for her culture and time. Elizabeth's red hair became popular after she was queen; Kardashian became a figurehead for the contouring trend. They and Wu perfected makeup trends that already existed to gain favor with those around them and attention from the public to put them near power in the first place.

Women who don't have the physical characteristics their culture deems stylish can use cosmetics and grooming to fit in instead. Like Kardashian's contouring illustrates, if a forehead is too big, makeup can make it look smaller. Lips can be made redder with lipstick, and powder can change the color of the face. Plastic surgery can actually change facial structure, and modern cosmetic procedures like Botox can be even easier on the body than surgery. Makeup and cosmetic procedures can also emphasize that a woman has money and time to spend and the prized knowledge of what is trendy—and time, money, and knowledge are essentially all that status encompasses.

Wu, Elizabeth, and Kardashian illustrate that in sexist societies, women not only have to understand cultural implications of cosmetics but must also be able to manipulate them to gain power they are not automatically granted. A woman's worth is so woven into her appearance that beauty and power can't be separated. Either beauty follows power, or power follows beauty. Trends change, and so do the methods used to achieve each society's version of what beautiful means. But that women in power generally need to emphasize wealth and youth remains consistent. Makeup is a way that women can portray the image they need to gain status, but its storied history makes the women who use it an easy target for men who claim those women are vain and shallow. This pattern happens time and time again: a beautiful woman gains power, then men turn her beauty against her once she loses that power. Until a woman can be valued for her personhood instead of appearance, this tug-of-war between beauty and power will remain.

THE COST
OF BEAUTY

Before the modern beauty industry, families in many cultures around the world often passed down recipes for face creams and other cosmetics, making makeup a family affair. People generally made cosmetics in kitchens instead of buying them in stores. Recipes for cosmetics were dispersed alongside recipes for cooking and medicines. Families would create recipe books they could pass down to children, or knowledge was traded among neighbors. Many central European families had their own recipes for face cream, often mixed on the kitchen stove then packed and preserved.

When Helena Rubinstein began selling face cream in 1903 in a business that grew to become a leading makeup company of her time, she created a family-focused narrative to help promote her product. She told customers she was importing her family's face cream from Poland. According to her myth, her family started using the cream on the recommendation of a close friend, the famous actress Modjeska, who had beautiful skin.[1] In reality, she produced the face cream Valaze in Australia, where she started her business, but she knew that selling the story of a family recipe was good marketing. She turned the idea of family traditions into a kind of currency to build her business, and being associated with Modjeska, who had luminous skin, was desirable.

This idea of a family unit honing a recipe over generations was a successful marketing tactic for Rubinstein. Women looking for reliable face creams seemed more willing to trust a family recipe based on the theory that what worked was passed onto the next generation and what didn't work wasn't—though that wasn't always true. Rubinstein capitalized on this popular belief to help build her brand.

Even as early as the sixteenth century, cosmetics tips and recipes were traded through letters, advice columns, and recipe books. A popular recipe book came from Caterina Sforza, a countess and member of the powerful Italian Medici family. Her book included hundreds of recipes, some of which were cosmetic, including ways to clear spots from the face, lighten skin tone, and remove wrinkles. Books like hers were popular with the wealthy and with women working as their servants who needed to know how to prepare and apply cosmetics to do their jobs. They were also popular with people who gained money and economic flexibility, who used products like makeup to show off their newfound wealth.

In many societies and cultures, makeup has long been used as evidence of wealth. The poor didn't have the time or money to spend on their appearance, but the wealthy could use servants or people they enslaved to aid them with toilettes—which, depending on the period and place, could be extensive. Following the trends of the upper class often required money. Makeup trends may change over time, but wealth has almost always dictated who can participate in fashion.

In the nineteenth and early twentieth centuries in Anglo-American societies, heavy makeup was *not* in fashion. Makeup generally had become the realm of women, and putting it on in public or wearing "too much" was considered gauche by polite society, which was overwhelmingly wealthy and white. In the dominant culture, beauty was deemed more valuable if it was natural—or if it appeared to be natural. Women who wore colorful, bold makeup, like ceruse or eye shadow, were often over-sexualized or distrusted by men and women alike. That didn't keep women from using concoctions to make their lips or cheeks rosier and their skin whiter—but women may have tried to hide it or be discreet about the products they used to benefit from being considered beautiful without the social risk of being known to wear makeup.

Around the early 1900s, cosmetics and hairstyling often were performed in the home for wealthy women in European and English societies. In the US, manicures and hairstyling would have likely been performed by lady's maids who helped with dressing. The realm of women was generally kept in the house instead of in public, and that included the process of getting dressed and putting on a public face. For wealthy white women in New York, that public face may have included rice powder and a hint of rouge on the cheekbones, along with lip balm and perfume.[2] Lady's maids could mix up cosmetics like face masks, bleaching creams, and powders to reduce shine.[3] Even if makeup wasn't put on in public, a well-groomed appearance—and hiring servants to help make that possible at home—was an indication of wealth.

Beauty is a form of currency, so we can be sure that communities based on cosmetic tips and tricks existed, even if they were kept somewhat out of sight. These discussions may have happened in whispers or in women-only spaces, like the women's section in the newspaper, but they formed the foundation of a tradition that would carry on as the open use of makeup cycled into fashion.

Makeup's public acceptance began to shift in the early years of the 1900s. One reason was the developing movie industry. Max Factor ran a salon and cosmetics manufacturer that sold the same makeup used to make faces expressive and beautiful on film. Actors would stop by Factor's building to be made up before heading to set, and the popularity of movies helped make makeup more common and acceptable.

Factor created bee-stung lips in the 1920s. He needed a process to apply lip color that would keep lip pomade from melting under the hot lights used during filming and affecting the greasepaint he used on the face.[4] He used his thumb to create two prints for the upper lip and one for the lower to create a heart shape, and then used a brush to paint the rest of the lips. This technique was first used on silent film star Mae Murray, but he also used it for Clara Bow.

And it was Bow, with her pouty lips and dark-rimmed eyes, who became a sex symbol and Hollywood's first It Girl. Bow's lips made lipstick look sexy and appealing, normalizing makeup use by making it visible and attractive to those able to see her films. Actors' appearances became commodities of their own. Not only were actors selling their image to appear in films, but their makeup looks also set trends that others followed by buying the same products or wearing makeup in the same way. Beauty companies also used actors as spokespeople or offered products to help one look the same as the women on screens, tying their profits to the popularity of movies.

Factor's salon served some of the biggest stars in Hollywood. In the salon, Factor created rooms for services based on people's coloring. There was a room for brunettes, blondes, what he called "brownettes" (light brown coloring between dark brunettes and blondes), and redheads. Instead of focusing on individual needs, Factor's strategy grouped women into categories meant to buy certain products. Similarly, Rubinstein created oily, dry, and normal categories for skin care to guide women's purchases. Dividing women into groups based on what products they should buy both gave women an identity—brunette, oily skin—and took it away. Instead of individuals with different needs, women were primed to consume as a group.

———

The opportunity to buy makeup and share tips with a community of like-minded women brought people together. What was once a private home practice grew into an excuse for many women to gather at the local salon. Within the first decade of the twentieth century, Factor, Madam C. J. Walker, Elizabeth Arden, and Rubinstein all opened salons. Other people ran beauty salons before, during, and since, but these businesses in particular had a great effect on the makeup industry—and therefore on US culture itself. Rubinstein,

Arden, Factor, and Walker did much to change the perception of using makeup. In doing so, they created socially acceptable communities around makeup and beauty and a market to buy it.

Throughout history, spas and baths have been social experiences for all genders, but they were not always connected to makeup and hairstyling. As modern industrial beauty companies took hold in the US and Europe, the process of getting made up became more public. During this transition period, many women remained wary of being seen wearing makeup or getting beauty treatments, but they still bought cosmetics and paid for services like facials from time to time.

Beauty salons weren't just about makeup but were about the entire process of constructing a physical self, including hairstyling, massage, and exercise. In a Rubinstein salon, a customer could get a milk bath, mineral bath, or herbal bath; an exercise room housed classes in stretching and posture; a doctor could provide a basal metabolism test; and facials, manicures, pedicures, and makeup lessons could round out the day.[5] In an Arden salon, services included hair and face treatments, body massage, and makeup application.

Rubinstein and Arden made their salons appealing to a high-society crowd that they were trying to cultivate in part by touring salons in Europe and bringing techniques they saw to their own businesses. The idea that treatments came from Europe made it easier for the wealthy to see salons as an exclusive, fashionable practice—just like fashions came from Europe, makeup could as well. A salon Rubinstein visited on her travels to spas around London had a discreet entrance for women who didn't want to advertise their treatments.[6] These secluded entrances created an almost secret society where people could let their guard down once they were inside. Like a clubhouse that had a password, they were only for those in the know.

The doors of Arden's salons, however, were painted a bright, shiny red. Instead of hiding the entrance the way some salons did, Arden's red door became a beacon. This door indicated the shift in public opinion surrounding women wearing makeup and wanting to openly associate with it. Instead of something to sneak into, it acted as an advertisement, welcoming people into the aspirational group allowed behind the door. Arden even used an image of her shiny red door in an advertising campaign. In one ad from 1939, Arden's red door floats against a white background. The door is encased in an arch with "Elizabeth Arden" written atop the doorframe. A smaller image of a woman's face wrapped in gauze appears to the right of the door. Her skin is flawless, her thin eyebrows arched, and her lips painted. Underneath is the phrase "Doorway to Beauty" and "For the world's fairest women."

Arden's Maine Chance—the US's first luxury health and beauty farm—took American salons to another level.[7] Guests could stay for an extended period, having health treatments in the morning and beauty treatments in the afternoon, along with outdoor sports like riding and tennis. The resort was an expensive, well-staffed place where women could diet, exercise, socialize, and beautify under Arden's strict regimens. In one photo from Maine Chance, four women all wearing matching white robes and exercise playsuits walk down a flight of stairs balancing books on their heads. Their hair is done, either curled or pulled back off their faces. Their deep painted lips contrast with their fair skin, all framed by thin eyebrows. The woman in the front has painted nails.[8] This resort created a community around beauty that one literally had to buy into. There was no way to participate without spending an exorbitant fee. Maine Chance created the luxury lifestyle that Arden hoped to cultivate for her customers. In doing so, she pushed for wellness and beauty to become things only those with money could buy. The resort was exclusive, but it offered community to those inside, making the beauty community a luxury item.

Arden helped create the image of the high-society white woman, and they were whom she wanted as customers. The salons added to the prestige of her brand, and the exclusivity of the expensive Maine Chance reinforced Arden's upscale clientele. It was to these wealthy women that Arden advertised her products, like the Montezuma red lipstick she created during World War II and the Saratoga red she advertised in 1963.[9] Every red lipstick she sold subtly harkened back to the door that enclosed the society within her salons. Wearing red lipstick alone could be a way to identify with like-minded women who were also interested in makeup—an advertisement similar to Arden's red door. With these signals, women created a community that supported and enabled their new makeup habits. But they could participate only if they paid to get in.

Wealthy white women weren't the only ones who wore makeup or who found community by sharing in beauty practices. Basically any culture that identifies with a certain appearance could use makeup to construct that appearance. Knowing what products to buy to follow the trends of a culture could be the ticket to be accepted into it.

For example, beatnik women in the 1950s likely used some of the same makeup as Arden's and Rubinstein's prime customers. Members of the Beat Generation sprang up around a literary movement of American authors like Allen Ginsberg and Jack Kerouac, whose work interrogated American culture and rejected materialism. When ideas from this counterculture spread into the mainstream, it became a fashion trend whose participants were known as beatniks. Beatniks wore heavy mascara and eyeliner, and they favored pale lips and dyed their hair white-blond or black. Rubinstein produced a package of hair dyes that became popular with beatniks. Beatniks and society women used the same tools but in a different way depending on what group they wanted to be in.

Deciding to participate in a trend like the beatniks meant finding like-minded people and identifying community members through their appearance, which often required money to spend on creating that appearance. Where the Beat Generation rejected materialism, participation in the fashion trend depended on buying the products and clothing to create the style. In this way, capitalism can distort the meaning of movements by tying consumption to communities.

Often, communities have their own look and forms of makeup application. It's more than a way of identifying members; constructing an appearance together is part of the intimacy of community and a kind of co-self-invention. This is evident in communities like drag, punk, and even cosplay. For many, these communities can act as a safe space, where people can create a sense of self and construct appearance away from the judgments of the dominant culture.

Around the same time Arden and Rubinstein were creating their salons, Black women like Walker were opening and running salons to serve Black women. These salons, which could be in their own shop or run out of someone's home, provided a place where Black women could create their appearance away from the white gaze. Arden and Rubinstein didn't focus on hair, though they did offer hairstyling. Clients at their salons generally wrapped their hair in turbans during treatments and often had maids at home to help dress their hair.[10] But Walker's and other Black women's salons generally did focus on hair, then added services like makeup and manicures. Salons and makeup provided methods of beautifying that became important touchstones for some Black communities. Beauty was seen as important for upholding and advancing Black people in society, and hair and beauty products were essential to this work.

Anthony Overton, who created the High Brown face powder—one of the first powders manufactured in the US to match Black women's skin tones—employed Black people who went door-to-door to sell his products. He eventually sold his products in certain department stores and drugstores as well. He used earnings from his company to become the primary underwriter of *Half-Century Magazine*, a publication for Black people that supported the women's club movement.[11] The magazine covered domestic topics like beauty and cooking alongside political stories and editorials. The first issue of the magazine in 1916 included information on the National Association of Colored Women and the National Republican Convention. It promoted Black-owned businesses and suggested that business and economic development were key in lifting up the race.

The issue also included beauty tips that emphasized the importance of beautiful skin. "Many of us have the idea that good clothes make us beautiful, but this is a mistake. What is a more disgusting sight than a woman dressed in fine clothes and in contrast her face showing a muddy, neglected and abused complexion," the magazine read.[12] Tips included how to clean and care for the skin and recommended using a good face cream to aid in moisturizing and removing blackheads. The beauty pages were written by Evelyn Northington, whom the magazine called a nationally renowned authority on beauty culture. The magazine recommended a complexion powder free of poisonous ingredients such as arsenic and white lead to help protect the skin from sun, dirt, and wind. Adorning these pages were advertisements for Overton's products, including peroxide vanishing cream and face bleach.

Beauty products helped to fund the magazine and helped Black people present themselves in a country filled with white people who judged them more harshly than they did other white folks. This beautifying could be seen as a form of political activism—and it required shopping to do it. Because the US operated (and still operates) under capitalism, even organizing to change politics took place under these same restraints—it had to be supported by independent wealth. In these cases, wealth was generated by beauty shops and buying and selling beauty products. Showing off that wealth in the form of made-up faces and hair also made some Black people feel they'd be more respected in a society dominated by whiteness.

Lucille Green Randolph was a beautician who did hair while also using her career in beauty to support political activism. Randolph was one of the first graduates of Walker's Lelia College of Beauty Culture in New York City, and she started her own salon.[13] She married political leader A. Philip Randolph and often supported him financially with her beauty-industry earnings. Both were members of the Socialist Party of the United States and worked to elect socialist politicians to local offices. Philip created the socialist newspaper *The Messenger*, and Lucille distributed the paper from her salon and sometimes paid off its debts.[14] Her beauty work made both her and her husband's political work possible and provided a space where she could control what was promoted and distributed.

Using Black beauty salons as hubs for organizing continued in the civil rights movement of the 1950s and '60s. Organizers distributed information about electing Lyndon B. Johnson in 1964 in various beauty shops. Activist Louis Martin put materials in beauty shops in five states, and he said that in those states they got a bigger vote.[15] "These efforts on the part of the NAACP and the Democratic National Committee were not dependent upon a savvy beautician, but the mere availability of a space frequented by a varied group of African American women that was hidden from those with a competing agenda," wrote Tiffany M. Gill in *Beauty Shop Politics: African American Women's Activism in the Beauty Industry.* The community that salons housed was important, not just for beautifying and companionship, but also for the opportunity to build a better life away from the eyes and influence of the dominant white culture. Even salons that didn't participate in direct political activity often provided a community space where people could meet and gather.[16] This provided essential space for Black communities to grow when recreational space was difficult for them to acquire.[17]

Beauty schools in the 1920s and '30s provided a place for recreational activities like sports and luncheons. The headquarters of the Apex News and Hair Company had a dance floor and a basketball court, the Poro College building held the headquarters for the National Negro Business League, and the Walker Company's building in Indianapolis became a kind of social and civic center.[18] Because beauty was profitable, the businesses associated with beauty had more freedom to make independent choices in a capitalist society. At the same time, these businesses and communities reinforced the profit seeking that capitalism requires. Gill writes that because of this, beauty salons housed contradictions. The salon visit was a personal, intimate experience in a social setting. It also provided rest while being the site of long, grueling days for its workers.[19] Like all businesses under capitalism, the opportunities that beauty provided came on the back of the workers. Community and respect had a price: the cost of a salon visit.

———

Communities also form around shopping and discussing which products to use. By the 1940s, Charles Revson had created seasonal product launches for Revlon, with makeup products tied to the fashion seasons of fall and spring, and other makeup companies followed suit.[20] This created a demand and a frenzy around the release of new products—the spectacle and anticipation created something to talk about. What new products were going to be a hit likely mattered to a woman who wanted to be fashionable, and many women wanted products that worked to deliver clear, youthful-looking skin even if they didn't keep up with seasonal trends.

With the invention of department stores, shopping became an especially social activity for wealthy white women in cities. Department stores became a place where women could spend the day eating and shopping, a small part of the world where they were expected to consume and exist the way men could anywhere. For those who didn't have access to larger stores, door-to-door sales provided an opportunity for an intimate conversation with a salesperson about the best products for someone's situation. These social shopping experiences set the stage for cosmetics shopping to be a communal activity—and that hasn't stopped. Shopping also gave women a socially acceptable way to be in public at a time when other public activities like working, politics, and education weren't welcoming or accessible. But this allowance was contingent on having money to shop. The stereotype that women love shopping and that shopping is a silly hobby makes fun of women for participating in the only leisure activity that was allowed to them when other options were closed off.

Working in the beauty industry was similar. When many industries wouldn't hire women, they were able to get jobs selling makeup because of its association with femininity. For many women, the makeup industry was a way to make independent money. Companies that hired women to sell door-to-door often emphasized that the role was compatible with being a wife and mother. The beauty industry's flexibility and openness to women employees created an opportunity, but it also locked women into working in that industry instead of finding other work.

Avon mainly employed women, though men were often hired for higher management positions in the company. Avon's door-to-door sales depended on the social nature of beauty sales and opened that social activity up for people who couldn't get to stores. The personal visit into the home provided a safe, intimate space to try on beauty products and discuss personal details about physical attributes like skin and hair but also emotional desires about appearance and aspirations. Avon founder David McConnell called the women he hired to sell Avon products "confidants."[21] One executive said that in Texas, salespeople had a hard time getting *out* of homes because they were offered cake and coffee.[22] Avon's sales were community based, creating community both for customers and among the sellers. Constant communication with the company and prize incentives made the sales representatives feel emotionally connected to their employer, and that connection lasted decades.[23]

The cosmetics industry—and its seasonal trends developed by Revlon—was set up particularly well for a continued relationship with a salesperson. Unlike other things sold door-to-door, such as books or vacuums, beauty products could be in relatively constant demand when next season rolled around.[24] In addition to making money from selling products, multilevel marketing companies like Avon allowed sellers to recruit new sellers and share in *their* profits. Multilevel marketing companies don't just sell makeup, they also sell clothing, jewelry, meal supplements, and more. Would-be salespeople—mainly women—became involved for many reasons: some women wanted a way to make money independently, some wanted flexibility at work, and some wanted to participate because it was fun. However, it could be difficult to sell enough to make a solid profit after buying the required supplies. These companies offer the incentive of communities, but it's tied to the worst part of capitalism: wealth is maintained at the top while workers may fall into debt trying to sell products.

Jane Marie, host of the 2018 podcast *The Dream*, talked with members of her family who have been involved in multilevel marketing companies for years. She recalled her grandmother selling Avon in the 1950s and going to selling parties for Avon in the '70s and '80s. Marie's aunt described the women at the parties as wearing heavy eye shadow and liner and a lot of hairspray. She recalled the smell of the Avon makeup and the warmth and laughter of the women. "These were wonderful gatherings—big to-dos in a town that didn't have much to do," Marie said.[25] Marie even remembered playacting being an Avon Lady when she was young, using the catalogs and makeup samples that were around the house. When these little girls played grown-up women, they pictured selling Avon. Avon selling parties provided social gatherings for women in small towns or rural areas, like where Marie lived with her family near Flint, Michigan. The community this provided was the main draw—but buying and selling makeup provided the reason to gather.

———

With the advent of the internet, beauty communities spread from salons or homes to virtual spaces, often including shopping for makeup. Location was no longer a barrier to discussing makeup products or techniques; parties could happen over comments instead of in someone's living room. The internet allowed communication between people no matter their location, widening the consumer market and the beauty community, just as door-to-door sales did for people who couldn't access larger stores.[26]

During the Cultural Revolution in China, many eschewed makeup and ornamentation as a sign of capitalism. Makeup was so representative of capitalistic tendencies in China at this time that to wear it was akin to supporting the system of capitalism itself. Makeup and skin-care products rose in popularity in China after reform and modernization in the 1980s, and products were generally more available and cheaper in bigger cities and coastal areas than in inland provinces, creating an opportunity for those who gathered online to share their resources.

In online communities, a certain method of online shopping emerged called *daigou*, where people in the community could buy what others couldn't find at all or couldn't find for a cheaper price then would mail the product to another person. The shopper would take a small commission from the sale to pay for time and labor. On the site OnlyLady, which had message forums for women on topics including makeup, clothing, love, interior design, family issues, health, and more, shopping arrangements sprang up as people shared recommendations and information on makeup and other cosmetics. The beauty product forum was more active than other forums on OnlyLady, highlighting that community and shopping for beauty products are deeply entrenched. Most of the women on OnlyLady who participated in daigou were middle-class women who worked in offices and wore makeup to work. In a study in the book *Chinese Women and the Cyberspace*, Gao Chong describes how the shopper accumulates social capital—and likely, more clients and more money—by answering questions about products.[27] Social networks and repeat customers also lessen the risk for the buyer by indicating that the person is trustworthy to complete the transaction.

At the heart of the daigou is sharing access to beauty products—and thus sharing the social and actual cost of beauty. Similar to salons, these women in online networks are helping each other become beautiful by sharing knowledge and time. Like any businessperson who depends on clients, social networks are key to this process. But because it's the beauty industry—which is based on subjectivity and personal insecurities, along with creativity and joy—the personal aspect of recommendations is important. Gao writes that some buyers find daigou more attractive than shopping in the streets alone because they trust the experience of the shopper and "cherish the feeling of being cared for."[28] OnlyLady had requirements to become a shopper, including being in the community for at least five months and being recommended by ten members who had been there at least three months. Outsiders to the community were not welcome to become shoppers in these transactions. Community had to come first, but that community couldn't be separated from consumption.

When buyers receive their products, they may post a photo of the item with words of praise or complaint. One user complimented the shopper on the transaction after she received the Avon products she ordered. She noted how carefully the items were wrapped with newspaper and attached a photo.[29] Every part of the shopping transaction can become a part of the community, from asking questions on what to buy to showing off the product after the purchase. There is no step or detail too small not to share.

Similar to a satisfied customer in a daigou, there is a genre of videos posted to social media called unboxing videos, where someone will post themselves opening a package to reveal the beauty products they received. These people share their shopping trip or online order as if with friends. Often they will sample the product and show swatches of lipstick or eye shadow on their skin or share a first impression of what it looks, feels, or smells like. Like daigou, these videos are sharing makeup that not everyone has access to. Beauty influencers especially have greater access to products than other people through brand partnerships, and they create a community around sharing that experience with people who can't spend the time or money to shop for these products on their own.

Beauty channels on YouTube can garner millions of followers, creating online communities based on certain influencers. Tati, a beauty YouTuber in the US who had over nine million subscribers as of summer 2020, regularly posts unboxing videos of makeup packages she receives from makeup companies. An unboxing video from January 2019 had nearly two million views. The twenty-five-minute video shows Tati and her husband sitting in front of a wall of packages, opening them one by one. Edited into the video are frames of close-ups on the unwrapped makeup products, brand name in full view. Tati sometimes showed how a product looks by swiping it in a thin line on the back of her hand and showing it to the camera. While opening the packages, Tati wears eye shadow from one of the companies that has sent her a box, her eyes glowing in an ombre green shadow that's brighter on the inside corner of her eyes, framed by thick black lashes. She pauses opening boxes to tell the viewers the name of the shadow she's wearing and says that she'll have a video up soon of her applying it.[30]

This unboxing video had more than one hundred thousand comments. There's a hunger to share experiences and talk about makeup and shopping. These videos provide a way to share knowledge and educate people who may never be able to afford or find certain designer products and want to see examples of drugstore products. Luxury brands could be tested and showed off alongside more affordable makeup options, mixing different price points and accessibility.

However, these videos, like capitalism itself, reinforce a hierarchy that keeps people with money at the top. There's no way to escape the fact that these communities are created to consume. It's difficult to become a leader in the community without the actual makeup products that people want to buy. Every video is related to discussions of whether products work or are worth buying; an unboxing video acts like an informercial for a variety of brands.

Makeup Alley, a site founded in 1999 to review and discuss products, created another group of devoted followers. Claire Carusillo wrote for Racked about consulting the site before shopping for beauty products to cross-reference people's recommendations. "No matter how much stuff you have, you'll keep coming back to the site to learn about the latest and greatest so you can buy even more," Carusillo said.[31] That's the heart of these online forums and communities. Buying new items fosters participation, which fosters buying more product. Consumption becomes community, and vice versa.

The barriers to entry for beauty communities have fallen with the rise in internet and social media use. More people can participate in some capacity regardless of their own personal budget or physical access to stores, in essence democratizing makeup communities. Money and location don't keep someone from becoming an expert in makeup application—though the people with the most power in these communities do have access to products, either by buying them or by receiving promotional items. Many online communities are free to enter—though access to the internet and a device to watch the video is required—and a person doesn't *have* to shop to watch, comment, or learn about makeup the way they often had to pay for a service to enter a salon.

This access has opened the world of makeup to a lot more people. Rubinstein's and Arden's carefully crafted wealthy white clientele are no longer the ones setting the trends or hoarding beauty knowledge behind hidden doors—the doors were broken down to allow anyone in. In addition, makeup companies are making more products with a wider shade range to include black and brown skin as well as white or light shades, and drugstore brands have increased the quality and number of products offered alongside luxury items. The global cosmetics industry (both skin care and makeup) has grown every year from 2004 to 2019; in 2019 it grew 5.25 percent.[32] Beauty companies are presumably happy to sell to more people, and more and more people have bought into the world of makeup.

As more people of all wealth levels—and races—have entered these communities, exclusivity shifted to maintain a hierarchy. In the late 2010s in the US, skin care became exponentially more popular than it had been in years past, with certain women forgoing makeup and opting for a "fresh face" that highlights perfect skin, without the help of full coverage foundation or other heavily pigmented products. Desirable products became expensive serums and lotions with fancy ingredients, along with procedures like Botox. Unblemished, smooth skin sans makeup—and the expensive facials and serums to get it—became a class marker.

Clear skin has always remained a fairly constant desire for those in the beauty community, but the amount of skin-care products and a jump in sales indicated a clear shift. Skin care was projected to increase by $20.1 billion between 2014 and 2019.[33] In early 2020, sales of skin-care products surpassed makeup for the first time, according to research firm NPD Group.[34] This shift is also reflected in media that documents and sets beauty trends. An article in *Vogue* from 2016 was titled "Skin Care Is the New Makeup: How to Go Barefaced and Love It"; a *New Yorker* headline from 2017 read "The Year That Skin Care Became a Coping Mechanism." An online subcommunity on the website Reddit called Skincare Addiction flourished.[35]

Instead of perfectly made-up faces, new products and treatments were created to idealize the best skin that money could buy. Krithika Varagur at *The Outline* called the skin-care craze a "reaction to the popular and populist aesthetic of contouring, the parallel universe of much-makeup makeup that's so big on Instagram and YouTube," while acknowledging that both looks take the same amount of products—which is to say, a lot.[36]

This emphasis on skin care was in part because of the globalization and expansion of communication about beauty. The Korean beauty industry had popularized extensive multistep beauty routines to achieve pristine, glasslike skin, and social media has spread knowledge of these routines to millennials and other younger consumers around the world who are more interested in skin care than their older counterparts. The strict skin-care regimens that originated with Korean women also caught on in white spaces in the US and became a trend. Heavy makeup cycles in and out of style, and with an influx of Korean skin care, heavy makeup was on its way back out in the US. Changing styles were built into the industry when makeup companies started releasing new products each fashion season; shifting beauty ideals could be seen as just another season of products to buy.

Just as in the beginning of the 1900s, women were again spending money and time on having a clear, smooth complexion without appearing to be wearing heavy makeup. But the effects of a made-up face are valuable even when the construction is hidden; the market for beauty exists even if it's impolite or awkward to be seen using it. Historian Kathy Peiss writes that beauty historically added value to women in patriarchal societies, whether they were enslaved, sex workers, or wives—and this remains true.[37] When a society sees women as commodities to be bought and sold, consumerism and capitalism become inextricable from womanhood and beauty.

TOOLS OF
RESISTANCE

Makeup trends may act as a vise, strictly holding women in place to enforce beauty standards the way a woodworker slowly and carefully shapes a block of wood into something smooth and perfect. But when people use makeup to break the system instead of conform to it, it can turn from a tool of the oppressor to one that strengthens the oppressed. That makeup tends to be associated with women means it can be a particularly strong touchstone for feminist protest. In addition, because makeup can be accessible or created at home, is such a bright visual signal, and is a flexible medium people can wear or remove as they choose, it can be an especially powerful form of resistance. A way to change society's standards—and therefore people's treatment in society when they don't fit into those standards—is to act out against them, and makeup can be a tool of resistance both when those standards have to do with appearance and when they don't.

In the years leading up to the Stonewall anti-police riots in 1969, makeup became both a target for law enforcement and a way to rebel against laws that restricted gendered appearance. A preexisting New York City law made illegal anyone "masked or in any manner disguised by unusual or unnatural attire or facial alteration," or anyone who congregated in a public place with people masked or disguised, except for authorized masquerade parties and parades.[1] The law was enacted in 1846 and was meant to prevent tenant farmers from protesting their landlords, which they sometimes did in disguise to hide from authorities.[2] In practice decades later, police used a guideline of enforcement of the law by targeting people wearing fewer than three pieces of clothing "appropriate to their sex" as a way to discriminate against LGBTQ people and businesses that served them.[3] By enforcing these laws in a way that reinforced straight cisgender society, police targeted those who didn't conform.

Because of discrimination from the police and the public, it was a risk for people to "appear" to be LGBTQ. Anyone who was gender nonconforming in their clothing, makeup, or hairstyling carried a risk of being confronted by police or turned away at businesses. But markers of makeup and clothing also helped LGBTQ people recognize each other and create (relatively) safe havens.

In the 1930s and '40s in New York, certain cafeterias on Christopher Street at Sheridan Square—near where the Stonewall Inn operated decades later—provided a place where gay men could publicly gather. At the Life Cafeteria, openly gay men, often styled with long hair and heavy makeup like blue eye shadow, mascara, and blush, would sit near the window, eating and talking. The business allowed this in part because of the crowds that would come to gawk at the people who flouted gendered expectations about appearance. Historian George Chauncey describes their makeup as one of the strategies gay men used to claim public spaces in the city. By emphasizing theatricality, they turned everyday locales into a stage, where breaking gender conventions was "less objectionable because it was less threatening."[4] The same way performers could get away with costumes that would be inappropriate offstage, these men intentionally overemphasized color and playfulness in their cosmetics to stage a sort of spectacle for straight onlookers who came to gawk.

Balancing playfulness with taking oneself seriously can be a dangerous line to walk—defying gendered expectations of appearance has always been risky, even under a guise of performance. Chauncey writes that people who did so were at higher risk of harassment from other customers, being kicked out of businesses, and arrest—especially when they didn't confine their appearances to places that tepidly tolerated them.[5] This is true in any decade: Desmond Vincent wrote for Very Good Light in 2020 about the risk of wearing cosmetics as a man in Nigeria, which has legalized systemic homophobia and where people can be arrested for just the suspicion of homosexual behavior. Vincent wrote about his decision to wear black nail polish in this environment. Police stopped him to question him about the nail polish, and he paid them money so they'd leave him alone. Later, a person on the street threatened him by reciting the anti-same-sex law. But he kept wearing the nail polish. "To me, painted nails means that I'm risking my life just to feel beautiful. And to that, I've realized this: Sometimes the most effective form of activism is simply daring to live. Not just exist, but truly, authentically and loudly, even when it seems illogical or risky to and goes against literal laws," he wrote.[6] For some, resistance can look like making oneself visible in a world that tries to erase the existence of LGBTQ people. Makeup, a visual signifier, can help make queerness visible.

In the 1960s, bouncers allowed people into the gay bar the Stonewall Inn based on their appearance—using appearance to define who was queer and who was deemed safe to let in. According to Chris Babick, a frequent customer, people working the door would look through a peephole, and "the man inside would look at you and, if you looked like you belonged there, would let you in."[7] Appearing effeminate by using clothing or makeup had been a way for gay men to identify each other for decades, including the men who wore makeup at the Life Cafeteria. Many gay men in the 1960s balanced an appearance that identified them as gay, likely with some elements of style that were gender-bending, with a conventionally masculine appearance that would allow them to safely navigate city streets. The customers allowed inside the Stonewall Inn made up a variety of subcultures within the LGBTQ scene in New York. Customers were primarily gay men, and the majority presented conventionally masculinely with no makeup.[8] Some dressed in a style of hippies, a growing subculture that had elements of gender-bending, with long hair, blue jeans, and floral or ruffled shirts. But a significant minority of the clientele represented bolder transgressions of straight white masculinity: scare or flame queens wore eye makeup and effeminate hairstyles but weren't necessarily attempting to "pass" as women, drag queens wore makeup and women's clothing to portray a character or persona, and some trans women wore makeup as part of their gender presentation. These customers were allowed in if their appearance passed the test at the front door.

The security measures that management at the Stonewall Inn used, like denying certain people entry if they "appeared" straight and having multiple locks and steel doors inside the outer oak doors, were meant to help protect the bar from police raids. When the bar was raided, the doorman would flip a switch that turned on bright white lights as a signal for those dancing and drinking inside. To combat officers attempting to get inside, the Stonewall doormen tried to recognize people's faces, along with judging their appearance, and asked potential customers to describe the inside of the bar to see if they had been before. Since admission to many gay bars and clubs depended on visual markers of belonging, police sometimes wore plainclothes in an attempt to get inside and raid them. On the night of the Stonewall raids, four male police officers wore dark three-piece suits and ties, a more conventionally masculine appearance than some of the Stonewall customers they were aiming to arrest.

The summer of the Stonewall riots, the police had ramped up their raids of gay bars in an attempt to close down the Mafia-owned establishments. In fact, they raided the Stonewall Inn on June 24 and came back a few days later, June 27, the night the riots erupted. Deputy Inspector Seymour Pine had put extra measures in place that night in an attempt to have more support to shut the Stonewall Inn down for good. This included women police officers who went undercover into the bar to help "examine" people dressed in clothing the police deemed feminine to determine if they "had undergone a sex change"—an assault on someone's body and privacy. If someone had gender-affirming surgery, they would not be arrested because they wouldn't be violating the gender roles the police proscribed that were based on external anatomy.[9] This enforcement shows that police officers felt they had authority over the bodies of LGBTQ people and that harassment and violation of their rights was a normal part of police work. Reflecting on this night years later, Pine said, "This was a kind of power that you have and you never gave it a second thought."[10] Police targeted those who violated gender norms, and men wearing drag were the first to be led into the paddy wagon outside the bar.[11]

One of the customers at the Stonewall Inn that night was Maria Ritter, a trans woman celebrating her eighteenth birthday. She had spent hours getting ready with her friend Kiki, wearing black stockings, a dress she took from her mother, and CoverGirl makeup she bought for herself, along with more makeup of her mother's. "It would take us hours, and at that time we painted for the gods: it would take us three or four hours to make up," she said in David Carter's 2004 book *Stonewall: The Riots that Sparked the Gay Revolution*.[12] Ritter also carried a purse with men's clothing in it in case she needed to change on the way home, likely to avoid harassment. That night at the Stonewall Inn, she didn't have a chance to change her clothes or wipe the makeup off her face. When Ritter saw police, she wanted to get out of the bar. As she went to the women's bathroom to see if it had a window, police ordered her to stand with other trans women and people dressed in a way the police deemed inappropriate for their gender.

The police didn't expect this vulnerable population to resist arrest—because they usually didn't. Historically, as today, police have felt empowered to abuse communities who lack the resources and societal support to fight for their rights in a justice system that's designed to support the status quo. That night at the Stonewall Inn, after tension had been building between the police and the LGBTQ community, people fought back, and riots continued for several days.

Marsha P. Johnson and Sylvia Rivera were trans women present at Stonewall the first night of the riots. They went on to start STAR, the Street Transvestite Action Revolutionaries, to provide housing and other support for trans youths in 1970. Both Johnson and Rivera did sex work throughout their lives, and both had been arrested repeatedly for sex work and for wearing women's clothing and makeup on the street. Rivera said that every time she was brought in front of a judge, they would say she was charged with "upper-head female impersonation"—so for wearing makeup and hairstyling that the dominant culture gendered as female.[13] In pictures of Johnson, she can be seen wearing flower crowns and red lipstick.[14] The blush high on her cheekbones and the color on her eyelids match her lipstick, as if she used the same product on her lips, cheeks, and eyes. And it's likely that she did because she didn't have much money to spend on cosmetics.[15] Johnson said she wasn't afraid of going to jail at the Stonewall riots because she had been going to jail for the past ten years "just for wearing a little bit of makeup down Forty-Second Street."[16]

Some LGBTQ activists responded to discrimination by emphasizing that gay people were just like straight people. "I had spent ten years of my life going around telling people homosexuals looked just like everybody else. We didn't all wear makeup and wear dresses," said Randy Wicker, who worked at the LGBTQ organization the Mattachine Society and later became friends and roommates with Johnson.[17] Wicker said that although he came around to be glad it happened, he was at first horrified by the uprising at the Stonewall Inn. "I thought at the time they were setting back the gay liberation movement twenty years, because I mean all these TV shows and all this work that we had done to try to establish legitimacy of the gay movement that we were nice middle class people like everybody else," he said.[18]

This way of thinking—that conforming to norms of the dominant culture will lead to better treatment of marginalized groups—is known as *respectability politics*. First defined by Evelyn Brooks Higginbotham in her 1993 book *Righteous Discontent: The Women's Movement in the Black Baptist Church* in the context of Black American history and Black churches, respectability politics can apply to a marginalized group that attempts to appeal to the dominant culture through manners, appearance, and behavior. While it may make sense on some level to prove to white straight folks that other people are humans too, just like them, the concept relies on policing members of a community to meet definitions and standards based on the white straight gaze. Narrowing what qualifies as "respectable" means narrowing who gets to go un-harassed in public. The definition of respectable in New York in the 1970s was generally based on straight culture and white cisgender people's bodies.

At this time, being "like everybody else" meant not wearing makeup unless one was a cisgender woman, and only wearing makeup that blended into what was trendy for white straight cisgender people. Not every LGBTQ person wore makeup, but people of all genders who bucked trends and gender expectations by using makeup faced a higher risk when in public. This is clear by the police targeting of trans women and others who wore feminine clothing and makeup during the Stonewall riots. It's also present in the activist movement that was born that night and often focused on white cisgender gay men while leaving out lesbians, bisexuals, trans women, and people of color—those who defied sexist and racist definitions of what was "respectable."

As trans women of color, Johnson and Rivera had to fight this battle over respectability and inclusion over and over. At a gay pride rally in 1973, Rivera made that point when she angrily addressed the crowd and asked them what they had done for the trans people in jail facing harassment and assault. At the rally, Rivera was kept from the stage for much of the day by organizers who ignored or disregarded her. When she finally did get on stage, she yelled into the microphone that she and the members of STAR were working for rights for everyone in the LGBTQ community—"all of us, and not men and women that belong to a white middle class white club."[19]

Later that night, disappointed at the lack of acceptance of her at the rally, she attempted suicide. She survived the attempt because Johnson found and helped her. Johnson was found dead in 1992, and though police said her death was a suicide, Rivera and others believed she was killed. The implications of who is deemed worthy of respect have violent consequences, which Johnson and Rivera knew because they were forced to see them.

By being in public, fighting for rights of all LGBTQ people no matter their gender, and demanding to be seen as who they were, Johnson and Rivera were trying to make the world safer for others, even when it wasn't safe for themselves. They refused to assimilate with standards that excluded women of color, trans people, and others who defied gender expectations. When they worked to expand LGBTQ rights, they did so in lipstick and eye shadow, emphasizing that makeup did not determine whether a person deserved safety and respect.

In Hong Kong in 2019, another law restricting makeup and masks led protesters to use makeup to defy police. In June of that year, mass protests broke out against a law that would have allowed extraditions to mainland China, which is governed by the Communist Party. A former British Colony, Hong Kong became part of China in 1997, though it was allowed to operate mostly independently from China's government under a policy called the Basic Law, which expires in 2047.

The protests escalated tension between the police and civilians, leading sometimes to violence. Police attacked the anti-government, pro-democracy protesters, firing rubber bullets and tear gas into crowds and beating people. Police stopped wearing identification badges, leading to increased protests because of the fear that police were attempting to avoid being reported for misconduct. The government also attempted to track protest leaders online, and protesters became wary that the government was using surveillance and facial recognition, which is prevalent in mainland China, to target participants in the protests. In response, many protesters wore masks to protect their identities and protect themselves from retaliation from police. The masks also helped protect the crowds from tear gas, should police use it. After months of protests, the government instituted a ban on masks and other face coverings. This difficult-to-enforce ban didn't stop protestors from wearing masks—or from using makeup to help disguise their faces.

One style of makeup that became prevalent is the face paint of the Joker character from Batman stories, which depicts white makeup on the whole face, with overdrawn, large red lips and sometimes a red nose, exaggerated red eyebrows, and blue eye shadow.[20] This makeup is meant to obfuscate people's faces and distort certain facial features to become unrecognizable on video surveillance. Where people who wore makeup became a target for police in New York amid anti-LGBTQ laws, protesters in Hong Kong used makeup in part to help protect themselves from becoming targets of police and facial recognition technology.

Protesters in Hong Kong aren't alone in using makeup to make surveillance more difficult. People in London and Moscow have also used face paint and makeup to confuse surveillance cameras and protest surveillance itself. In London in 2020, people made themselves up in the style of dazzle camouflage in World War I, which uses asymmetrical patterns in contrasting colors and sharp lines to make depth difficult to read. People in Moscow similarly used bold, bright asymmetrical designs to attempt to confuse cameras. By disguising their faces in this way, people can remain safer and the protest movement can continue by protecting participants from technology that would identify them. It becomes tool for longevity—a way to maintain the fight.

Directly defying laws about appearance can push for political change. It also forces the government to deal with how certain laws are enforced, leading to either a tightening or a loosening of restrictions. In North Korea, the government used rules around makeup to control and suppress people—makeup became an agent of the state. Actor Nara Kang fled North Korea in 2015 because the government restricted her personal freedoms, including what makeup she could use. She said to CNN in a 2020 article that most people in her North Korean hometown were only allowed to wear a light color on their lips, maybe a pink but never red: "Whenever I put on makeup, older people in the village would say that I'm a rascal smeared with capitalism," recalls Kang. "There was a patrol unit every 10-meters to crackdown on pedestrians for their looks."[21]

Defectors from North Korea told CNN that wearing clothes deemed as "too Western" would lead to fines, public humiliation, or punishment like hard labor, but the rules could vary in different regions.[22] In Pyongyang, university students acted as disciplinary officers called *Daehaksaeng gyuchaldae*, and they mainly target women and enforce rules about appearance, like approved hairstyles and lipstick colors.[23]

Rules about appearance may seem frivolous for a government to care about and enforce, but by asserting control over appearance, the government maintains control over its people. Enforcing dress codes prevents individual self-expression and represses personal agency while creating an excuse to increase the government's surveillance of its citizens. The Daehaksaeng gyuchaldae are watching—not just for brightly colored lipstick but also for behavior, speech, and other outward markers of rebellion or disobedience.

Some people in North Korea wear styles of makeup they are exposed to by watching DVDs of bootleg versions of Western television shows, for sale in black markets. By seeing beauty trends from outside North Korea then wearing those trends, people show others that they are willing to resist the government and at least break these small rules—first viewing illicit entertainment, then buying and wearing illicit cosmetics based on that entertainment. In this way, makeup becomes a symbol of rebellion and a signal to encourage others to expand the culture of North Korea.

To take care of one's own body and decide how to adorn it is to practice exercising choice and attention. Following fashion trends can reveal a person's values, interests, and emotions. When that is removed and replaced with direction from the government, people pay attention to the government instead of themselves. Nation-building in other regimes around the world have also associated "unity with uniformity" and attempted to remove the *appearance* of inequality by forcing citizens to dress similarly.[24] But focusing on appearance instead of the underlying structure of society doesn't remove actual inequality; it creates an additional burden.

———

Conformity to a certain appearance is also present in societies with governments that don't regulate dress, because culture provides its own set of rules. Kang defected to South Korea, which offered her the freedoms she couldn't have in North Korea. Ironically, Kang arrived soon before some South Korean women were championing an "escape the corset" movement that encouraged women to destroy their cosmetics, cut their hair, and remain barefaced. The movement protested the long hours and amounts of money that women spend to keep up with the culture's beauty standards.

In the 2010s, the look the majority of South Korean society deemed preferable included clear, smooth, glowing skin; blush high on the apples of the cheeks; a heart-shaped face; long hair; and big eyes with long eyelashes to give the impression of a "baby-faced appearance."[25] To achieve this, women spend hundreds of dollars a month and many hours a day. "We go through 12 steps just to put on the basic products before we even apply makeup," said Kim Ji-yeon to the *New York Times* in 2018.[26] Kim estimated she spent two hundred dollars a month and two hours a day on her appearance; another woman who spoke to the *New York Times* estimated she spent seven hundred dollars a month. Plastic surgery to achieve the "right" look is a booming industry in South Korea—Kim had double jaw surgery, a procedure to break the jawbone and realign it, and a popular procedure called double-eyelid surgery that adds a crease to the eyelid to make eyes look bigger. Although statistics are difficult to gather because it's unregulated and there aren't records, some estimates say that, as of 2015, between one-fifth and one-third of women in the capital city of Seoul have had plastic surgery.[27]

Yim Hyun-ju, a television news anchor at the Munhwa Broadcasting Corporation, became involved in the escape the corset movement perhaps inadvertently when she wore her glasses on a broadcast in April 2018. Her false eyelashes had been making her eyes tired, and she was using a bottle of artificial tears each day.[28] In response, her producers reprimanded her and some viewers complained—but some women *thanked* her. She said she didn't want to be part of any movement, but she does wear her glasses from time to time in part to send a message to viewers to judge her on her competence and not her appearance. "If I could act freely, I would apply makeup less," she said.[29]

There are no laws that enforce Yim's use of makeup. Rather, her treatment in the world and at her job pushes her to act and look a certain way. If she hadn't worn her glasses, she wouldn't have been reprimanded; doing so put her job at risk. Wearing glasses may seem like a small choice for a person in their everyday life, but when it could affect income, safety, and health, it becomes a huge decision. Every small decision becomes a big decision when it goes against what's protected in the mainstream.

The women breaking away from these standards in South Korea are prioritizing their health and independence over their appearance, and their protests ask that others do the same. The escape the corset movement uses bold visual signals to remind others to reject whatever aspects of mainstream culture don't serve them. Becoming a part of a new subculture trend provides strength and solidarity to those fighting back. Like bright lipstick in North Korea, this pointed lack of makeup, short haircut, and glasses shows the world that personal style is a possibility, no matter how powerful or threatening the dominant culture may be. Like Johnson and Rivera and others who act out against oppressive standards of appearance, these activists reinforce the power that stems from thoughtful individualism. When people have the space to express themselves in ways that deviate from trends or strict beauty standards, standards expand for others to do the same without fears of harmful repercussions.

———

The feminist movement in the US has similarly protested makeup and standards of beauty at different times as part of the fight to expand women's rights. Each wave of feminism has come to be associated with a different response to makeup as images of respectability and protest have shifted over decades. Makeup—and people's feelings about it—became a marker of being for or against the feminist movement.

A rumor in years since the first wave of US feminist activism claimed that leaders of the suffragette movement in the US and UK in the early 1900s, like Elizabeth Cady Stanton and Emmeline Pankhurst, wore lipstick to suffrage parades to shock the crowds and protest the way women were treated in society. In reality, the white leaders of the suffragette movement often focused on respectability—which, in the early 1900s in the UK and US, meant *not* wearing makeup.

But the suffragettes did focus on beauty. In the US especially, suffragettes wanted to show that being a feminist didn't equate with being "unwomanly," so they emphasized dominant ideas of feminine beauty in their protests to try to gain more support from those who were outside the feminist movement. At this time, this meant white, bare skin (or at least no visible makeup), long straight hair, and fashionable clothing, hats, and jewels.

Ultimately, though, this version of acceptable womanhood left out women of color and others who didn't fit into what was seen as respectable. In the 1913 suffragette march in Washington, DC, organizer Alice Paul encouraged people to essentially ignore Black women because "the participation of negros would have a most disastrous effect" on the white women from the South who already agreed to participate.[30] The National American Woman Suffrage Association decided to segregate the event, asking Black suffragettes to march at the end of the parade instead of walking with the delegations from their states. The organizers did this so as not to ruin the image of acceptability white suffragettes were trying to impart. After telegrams, protestations, and women like Ida B. Wells-Barnett objecting to this segregation, Black women marched according to their states and occupations.

In the second wave of feminism in the US, women actively spoke out against beauty standards they viewed as harming women. At a protest of Miss America in 1968, the group New York Radical Women aimed to publicize critiques of women's oppression. As part of the protest, the women had a "freedom trashcan" in which they threw objects that harmed women and contributed to their oppression. Items in the trash can included hair curlers and false eyelashes.[31] Protesters also carried signs opposing "the degrading mindless-boob-girlie symbol" and saying that a free woman "is no longer enslaved by ludicrous beauty standards."[32] One sign said, "Can make-up hide the wounds of our oppression?"[33] In this protest, a lack of makeup was defiance against the standards that had come to define respectability and beauty for women.

This protest became known for its "bra burners"—though there were no bras actually burned. Participants discussed a symbolic bra burning, and the rumor that they were really set on fire persists. This rumor haunted the feminist movement for years. Opponents used the image of bra burning and trashing makeup to trivialize what feminists were asking for. Activist Carol Hanisch, who was part of the New York Radical Women, made popular the phrase "the personal is political" to emphasize that women's personal choices were born from their status as oppressed people. Opponents of the feminist movement twisted this meaning to suggest that women were making purely personal choices about self-presentation and that systemic oppression couldn't be affecting those decisions. The idea that women were complaining about their comfort or about makeup—and therefore their vanity—was used as evidence that feminists didn't need to be taken seriously.

Using items that are gendered as female to minimize what feminists were arguing for was a way to build upon people's already existing sexist views that femininity itself is trivial. Radical feminists were dismissed as manly, ugly, and forever single because of their rejection of the things that made up white, straight, mainstream definitions of conventional womanhood. For the suffragettes, not wearing makeup was a mark of proper womanhood; for radical feminists in the second wave, not wearing makeup was a *rejection* of proper womanhood. Women are so tightly bound to the things that make up their appearance that there is no way to address women's rights without addressing beauty standards and how women navigate them. The struggle becomes getting the dominant culture to take appearance politics seriously and to understand how it affects the lives of women every day, instead of dismissing it as frivolous and vain.

Some modern feminists are pushing back on the idea that "girly" things, like makeup and bras, are automatically inferior. "The third wave would go on to embrace all kinds of ideas and language and aesthetics that the second wave had worked to reject: makeup and high heels and high-femme girliness," wrote Constance Grady in Vox in 2018.[34] Embracing makeup and its association with femininity became a way to embrace womanhood and assert that women deserved rights whether they wore lipstick or not. Feminist writer Chimamanda Ngozi Adichie became a brand ambassador for makeup company No. 7 in 2016, and when she agreed to the role, she decided she wanted to be a part of the message that women who like makeup also have serious things in their lives—that one doesn't negate the other. "I think it's time to really stop that ridiculous idea that somehow if you're a serious woman you can't and should not care about how you look," she said.[35]

In this cultural context of reimagining what makeup can mean to women, not wearing makeup can still create a powerful message of resistance to cultural norms. In 2016, singer Alicia Keys decided to no longer wear makeup after a photographer asked to shoot her without it and she realized she felt more comfortable and beautiful without it.[36] Keys wrote that she felt she had been hiding behind makeup and changing who she was to be accepted in society. Penelope Green described the backlash to Keys's decision: "#Nomakeup was empowering and brave. No, it was annoying, incendiary and invasive. Ms. Keys's (mostly female) detractors howled at her disingenuousness (surely she had spent thousands on skin care?) and her deceit (surely she was wearing tinted moisturizer?); some slammed her for not looking pretty enough (though they used coarser words than those)."[37] Certain judgments follow women around whether they wear makeup or not, love it or hate it, reject it or accept it. For Keys, not wearing makeup was a way to reject cultural norms that bound her. For some, her rejection of makeup was a hypocritical rejection of womanhood itself.

Keys has privileges like fame and money that likely help her receive other benefits—like clear skin and groomed eyebrows—that help her withstand the social consequences of not wearing makeup. Other women may not have the cultural or political power to defy norms like not wearing makeup without a bigger risk to their economic and social well-being.

But Keys is a Black woman celebrity, and her decision doesn't come without risk to herself. She faces racism in a country that prioritizes whiteness in beauty. Defying norms to make a statement on how those norms affect women's lives has a higher risk of alienating herself from her business and fans than many white women would face. Who wears makeup—and who can afford not to—is inextricably linked to race and class. When Keys broke ranks with the dominant culture's ideals of what a woman should be, it forced people to reckon with what wearing makeup means, similar to the protest at the Miss America pageant years before. "Alicia Keys could be taking a page from the no-makeup orthodoxy of the women's movement 40 years ago," said feminist activist Letty Cottin Pogrebin.[38] Tactics have changed over the years, but makeup is still a touchstone for feminist protest, and it will likely remain so until makeup is no longer associated with women's worth—or womanhood itself.

—

Makeup—or a lack of it—can be a good way to force a confrontation with society because it's a visual signal, like a protest sign for the face. Red lipstick especially has a history of being a powerful symbol—of sexuality, of confidence, of patriotism, and more—that has indicated different values and priorities for the wearer.

In April and May 2018 in Nicaragua, protesters demonstrated against President Daniel Ortega's fiscal reforms that raised taxes and cut social security. His administration's response to the 2018 protests was violent, with Amnesty International reporting that the state killed more than seventy people, with hundreds more injured.[39] For the next few years, protestors gathered to demonstrate against Ortega's continued violence and imprisonment of people who spoke out against the government.

When journalist Marlen Chow protested the Nicaraguan government in October 2018, she wore red lipstick, as she said she always does when she goes to a protest.[40] At this protest, police violently arrested thirty-eight people, including Chow. "The torture starts from the moment they grab you," Chow said in an interview on independent news site Confidencial.[41] When the police interrogated Chow about her involvement in the protest, she said she "took an air of sarcasm to the interrogation."[42] When the police asked what organization she belonged with, Chow said she took out her lipstick and gave it to the other women she was with and they put it on as best they could while restrained. "We are the association of Nicaraguan women with red lipstick," she said.[43]

Since then, red lipstick has become a way for the public to show their disapproval of the administration and solidarity with political prisoners. People of all genders have posted pictures on social media of themselves wearing red lipstick. Posting these pictures keeps the protest movement alive without putting people at risk of arrest for publicly gathering to protest. Red lipstick became a symbol of peaceful protest, in contrast with the red blood spilled by the state.

Chow said that her inspiration came from Nicaraguan–Salvadoran writer Claribel Alegria, "who founded the Association of Nicaraguan Women of Red Lips."[44] Alegria was an essayist, poet, and journalist who spoke out for social justice and freedom in Latin America. Although Chow didn't mention the story Alegria wrote called "Granny and the Golden Bridge," it references both makeup and rebellion against the government. In the story, a grandmother brings food to Salvadoran state troops guarding a bridge during a civil war. However, the grandmother provided more than food—she also helped to bomb the bridge and supplied ammunition to the guerrilla group opposing the government. After the bridge exploded, the grandmother dyed her hair red and put on lipstick, posing as the owner of a brothel. When she was made up to appear like a younger woman, she wasn't recognized by the soldiers who suspected her of the crime and came looking for her.

It's in this spirit that Chow and her supporters also wear red lipstick. The lipstick becomes a subversive tool to oppose the government's actions. A history of beauty contests in Latin America have reinforced strict gender roles where women represent gentle beauty, in contrast with the machismo of Latin American men. Claiming lipstick as a political tool upends the expectation that women stay silent, beautiful, and accommodating. "It's like they were so disconcerted to see that we were really speaking out against their aggression," Chow said about her arrest.[45] Men participating in the protest by wearing lipstick also go against expectations for them to eschew what is typically deemed feminine. These visual contrasts add the weight of defiance to the protest, and speaking out with their actions as well as their appearance can give the protestors strength.

That lipstick is common is partly what makes it so ideal as a protesting tool. Chow had it with her when she was arrested—she also wore it in the interview about her arrest. It would be unrealistic, maybe impossible, to arrest everyone who carried it. An individual alone wearing red lipstick may not arouse suspicion, and a person could avoid association with the protests by not wearing lipstick until it begins and removing it when it's over. Along with protesting by posting photos on social media, people have organized some flash protests, where protests disband after a few minutes, before the police can take action against them. Nicaraguan police have banned signs of opposition to the government and the use of patriotic symbols. Red lipstick is a common item made uncommon by its use; it's not a symbol of opposition until it's used to oppose. Using lipstick in this way almost divorces it from beauty or class. It instead becomes a visual marker of independence, rebellion, and justice.

Instead of using makeup to indicate status or emphasize beauty, makeup can become a way to fight for recognition and safety. In 2015 in Mexico, women used makeup to raise awareness of and protest the high murder rate of women in the country. Women's groups in Mexico used performance to embody the women who were killed. One street theater performance included women yelling the names of the murdered women as the mother of one of the victims yelled, "Help me, help me," while holding a sign adorned with her daughter's photo. Manuel Amador, the founder of Redefem Edomex, an organization to denounce femicide, said, "The state reports on these women's deaths, just saying there is another dismembered body, or another body dumped in a garbage bag. . . . We don't hear their stories, so that's why we have to fill our performance with their humanity."[46]

Makeup, and the effort it takes to put it on as part of a performance, brought the performers and the audience closer to an understanding of the violence these girls and women face. The makeup
these women used in their performances honored the memory of
the murdered women by showing the effort they put into embodying their pain and humanity. One woman used glittery eye shadow
as part of her performance, embodying a sense of playfulness and
fun these murdered women should have had the chance to experience.[47] In this protest, the women screamed the names of those who
were killed, and their bold makeup visually reflected this: They were
screaming with both their words and their appearances. Items like
lipstick and glitter are also gendered—and these women specifically
protested violence against women. In doing so, they used accessible
tools in new ways.

The malleability of makeup is important when it comes to protesting.
Makeup is like ink that can be used to write any message, depending on the culture, context, and use. The same makeup on different
people can mean different things at different times, either strength-
ening or hurting certain causes.

During the Boston Tea Party, American colonists appropriated
the image of Indigenous Americans as part of their protest, misusing
a symbol in a racist way to create an image of rebellion. To protest
a tax on tea, a group of American colonists boarded ships in Boston
Harbor and dumped hundreds of chests of tea into the water, esca-
lating political tensions between the colonies and the British government. Some of the colonists wore paint on their faces in a crude
impersonation of people belonging to the Mohawk tribe. Colonist
George Hewes remembered using coal dust from a blacksmith's shop
to blacken his face.[48] The disguise partly hid the colonists' faces and
identities, but they likely chose to paint their faces in this way specifically to evoke stereotypes about Indigenous Americans. Many white

settlers saw Indigenous Americans as uncivilized savages and viewed the paint they wore on their bodies as indicative of their lower status. This is a false, racist belief—they didn't take the time to learn or understand what the paint may have meant or respect the people using it. To protest their own government—which murdered and colonized Indigenous Americans—these white colonists took an image out of context from a culture that wasn't their own to appeal to the racist white gaze that viewed the paint as rebellious. Using paint in this way indicated a lack of understanding and appreciation for the symbols and relied on racism to get their message across.

In modern times, people in certain Indigenous cultures wear paint in new ways that reclaim symbols and don't rely on stereotypes. What became known as "war paint" in white society is not so much about war as it is about ceremony, wrote Ruth Hopkins, a Dakota/Lakota Sioux writer.[49] And in the twenty-first century, she wrote, some Indigenous Americans are using paint to create new conventions. Indigenous people in control of their own representation have worn paint at the 2020 Women's March in Washington, DC, and at protests fighting climate change. A red handprint over the mouth has become a particular symbol to bring awareness to the Missing and Murdered Indigenous Women movement. Reinventing the meaning of paint and wearing it in new ways can also be a part of revitalization of Indigenous American cultures—an act of resistance in itself when white people have misused and appropriated those images as a form of destruction.

When there are rules and assumptions that govern appearance— either set by the government or the dominant culture—breaking those rules can push for change and bring attention to a protest. Makeup is visual and can be used to create a symbol of resistance, but makeup alone doesn't have meaning until people ascribe meaning to it. Suddenly, such a little tool can mean the difference between acceptance and defiance, independence and conformity, and, sometimes, life and death.

ACKNOWLEDGMENTS

Thank you to my agent, Sarah Phair, for believing in this idea and supporting it even when it changed shapes. I'm so glad to have you on my team. Thank you to my editor, Haley Lynch, who was excited about this book from the start and whose contributions and sharp editing were so valuable in making *All Made Up* what it is. Thank you also to Helene Atwan, who saw the potential in this book and helped make sure it landed at Beacon. The entire team at Beacon has been wonderful, including Raquel Pidal, Susan Lumenello, and Marcy Barnes, who made copyediting, proofs, and all of production an easy and welcoming process. Emily Powers and Perpetua Charles, thank you for your hard work on marketing and publicity. Thank you to Carol Chu, who designed the beautiful cover. I have felt supported every step of the way.

Laura Bullard, thank you for your astute fact-checking. Fact-checking is an intimidating process, but with you it was less so. Any error in this book is my own.

Thank you to all librarians everywhere, especially those who work at Sulzer Regional Library and who filled all of my interlibrary loan requests. There are too many to list, but thank you to everyone who answered my research questions over emails and phone calls during a pandemic—your contributions made this book stronger. You didn't have to take the time, and I appreciate that you did.

Thank you to Ipsita Agarwal, my friend and virtual coworker while writing this book. Thank you to the members of my writing group: Ines Bellina, Lindsay Eanet, and Rosamund Lannin. Your company, advice, and support are treasured. Thank you to everyone in my group chats—you know who you are.

Thank you to my parents, who support me always and who encouraged reading and writing my entire life, even when I didn't know yet that I wanted to be a writer. Thank you to my dad specifically for getting me a book every time I was interested in something and to my mom for making me look up words in the dictionary when I was young, even when I was annoyed about it.

To my husband, Michael, thank you for your endless support and love, which made this book possible. You did so many dishes while I was on deadline and gave me so many hugs when I was stressed. I appreciate it all.

NOTES

INTRODUCTION

1. Tressie McMillan Cottom, *Thick: And Other Essays* (New York: New Press, 2019), 44.

2. Fenty Beauty by Rihanna, "New Year's Eve Makeup Look With Amandla Stenberg," December 8, 2019, video, 2:50, https://www.youtube.com/watch?v=x8HFdA1asgM.

3. Vogue, "Lucy Hale's 25-Step Guide to Everyday Makeup," June 18, 2020, video, 13:30, https://www.youtube.com/watch?v=BmAmQct3BJc.

4. Simone Weichselbaum, "Fakeup," Marshall Project, November 19, 2014, https://www.themarshallproject.org/2014/11/19/fakeup.

5. Joan Potter, "County Prisoners Escape Uniformity," *New York Times*, September 25, 1977, https://www.nytimes.com/1977/09/25/archives/new-jersey-weekly-county-prisoners-escape-uniformity-inmates-escape.html.

6. Marlen Komar, "Why Makeup Matters to Women in Prison," Racked, January 3, 2018, https://www.racked.com/2018/1/3/16797784/makeup-prison.

7. "Vanity, Too, Laughs at Locksmiths," *Mitchell Capital*, February 7, 1908, https://chroniclingamerica.loc.gov/lccn/sn2001063112/1908-02-07/ed-1/seq-12.

8. Komar, "Why Makeup Matters to Women in Prison."

9. Kathy Peiss, *Hope in a Jar: The Making of America's Beauty Culture* (Philadelphia: University of Pennsylvania Press, 2011), 182.

10. Jia Tolentino, "The Age of Instagram Face," *New Yorker*, December 12, 2019, https://www.newyorker.com/culture/decade-in-review/the-age-of-instagram-face.

11. Adam Rhew, "Why Local News Anchors All Have the Same Look," Racked, February 1, 2017, https://www.racked.com/2017/2/1/14441128/local-news-anchor-image-consultants.

12. McMillan Cottom, *Thick*, 72.

13. Kathy Peiss, "On Beauty . . . and the History of Business," *Enterprise & Society* 1, no. 3 (September 2000): 485–506, http://www.jstor.com/stable/23699594.

14. Elisabeth Sherman, "Meet the Teenage 'Beauty Boys' Coming for the Cosmetics Industry," *Guardian*, July 20, 2020, https://www.theguardian.com/lifeandstyle/2020/jul/20/beauty-boys-men-makeup-teenagers-cosmetics-industry.

15. Katy Kelleher, "Ugly Makeup: The Trend Highlighting What's Beyond Conventional Beauty," *Guardian*, May 8, 2020, https://www.theguardian.com/fashion/2020/may/08/ugly-makeup-trend.

WORKING IT

1. Nancy L. Etcoff et al., "Cosmetics as a Feature of the Extended Human Phenotype: Modulation of the Perception of Biologically Important Facial Signals," *PLOS ONE* 6, no. 10 (October 3, 2011), https://doi.org/10.1371/journal.pone.0025656.

2. Mindy Isser, "The Grooming Gap: What 'Looking the Part' Costs Women," *In These Times*, January 2, 2020, http://inthesetimes.com/article/22197/grooming-gap-women-economics-wage-gender-sexism-make-up-styling-dress-code.

3. Rebecca Nash et al., "Cosmetics: They Influence More Than Caucasian Female Facial Attractiveness," *Journal of Applied Social Psychology* 36, no. 2 (2006): 493–504, https://doi.org/10.1111/j.0021-9029.2006.00016.x.

4. Jaclyn S. Wong and Andrew M. Penner, "Gender and the Returns to Attractiveness," *Research in Social Stratification and Mobility* 44 (April 2016): 114, https://doi.org/10.1016/j.rssm.2016.04.002.

5. Julia Carpenter, "How a Woman's Appearance Affects Her Career," CNN Money, September 20, 2017, https://money.cnn.com/2017/09/20/pf/women-attractiveness-work/index.html.

6. Melissa Dahl, "Stop Obsessing: Women Spend 2 Weeks a Year on Their Appearance, TODAY Survey Shows," *TODAY*, February 24, 2014, https://www.today.com/health/stop-obsessing-women-waste-2-weeks-year-their-appearance-today-2D12104866.

7. SWNS, "Vanity Costs American Women Nearly a Quarter of a Million Dollars," *New York Post*, July 6, 2017, https://nypost.com/2017/07/06/vanity-costs-american-women-nearly-a-quarter-of-a-million-dollars.

8. "Black Impact: Consumer Categories Where African Americans Move Markets," Nielsen, February 15, 2018, https://www.nielsen.com/us/en/insights/article/2018/black-impact-consumer-categories-where-african-americans-move-markets.

9. Wong and Penner, "Gender and the Returns to Attractiveness," 114.

10. Doreen Pierre, "The Problematic Politics of Style and Gender Identity in the Workplace," HuffPost, September 12, 2019, https://www.huffpost.com/entry/style-gender-identity-workplace_1_5d711924e4b09bbc9efab37c.

11. Priya-Alika Elias, "What Does Dressing 'Professionally' Mean for Women of Color?," *Vox*, March 8, 2018, https://www.vox.com/2018/3/8/17096202/women-poc-office-dress-code-professional-attire.

12. Anthony J. Mayo, Masako Egawa, and Mayuka Yamazaki, "Yoshiko Shinohara and Tempstaff," Harvard Business School Case 409-049, March 31, 2011, 5.

13. Mayo, Egawa, and Yamazaki, "Yoshiko Shinohara and Tempstaff," 5.

14. Kyodo News via AP Images, "Tempstaff to Integrate Management with People Staff," April 17, 2008, http://www.apimages.com/metadata/Index/Tempstaff-to-integrate-management-with-People-Staff/3e64f218dc9142029960849cff9a416d/2/0.

15. Kumiko Nemoto, *Too Few Women at the Top: The Persistence of Inequality in Japan* (Ithaca: Cornell University Press, 2016), 132.

16. Nemoto, *Too Few Women at the Top*, 5.

17. Nemoto, *Too Few Women at the Top*, 132.

18. Nemoto, *Too Few Women at the Top*, 139.

19. Nemoto, *Too Few Women at the Top*, 138.

20. Nemoto, *Too Few Women at the Top*, 138.

21. Emily Yellin, *Our Mothers' War: American Women at Home and at the Front During World War II* (New York: Free Press, 2004), 39.

22. Yellin, *Our Mothers' War*, 39.

23. Sarah Myers and G. Kurt Piehler, "How One 'Rosie the Riveter' Poster Won Out Over All the Others and Became a Symbol of Female Empowerment," The Conversation, May 25, 2018, https://theconversation.com/how-one-rosie-the-riveter-poster-won-out-over-all-the-others-and-became-a-symbol-of-female-empowerment-96496.

24. Yellin, *Our Mothers' War*, 59.

25. Lindy Woodhead, *War Paint: Madame Helena Rubinstein and Miss Elizabeth Arden: Their Lives, Their Times, Their Rivalry* (Hoboken, NJ: John Wiley & Sons, 2003), 287.

26. Sarah Jane Downing, *Beauty and Cosmetics 1550–1950* (Oxford, UK: Shire Publications, 2012), loc. 830, Kindle.

27. Maureen Honey, *Creating Rosie the Riveter: Class, Gender, and Propaganda during World War II* (Amherst: University of Massachusetts Press, 1984), 6.

28. Kathleen M. Barry, *Femininity in Flight: A History of Flight Attendants* (Durham, NC: Duke University Press, 2007), 3.

29. Mark Ellwood, "I Was a Flight Attendant During the Golden Age of Travel," *Condé Nast Traveler*, June 6, 2019, https://www.cntraveler.com/story/i-was-a-flight-attendant-during-the-golden-age-of-travel.

30. Rick Seaney, "Did They Really Wear Girdles? Q&A with a Former Pan Am Stewardess," ABC News, October 12, 2011, https://abcnews.go.com/Travel/wear-girdles-qa-pan-stewardess/story?id=14720587.

31. Barry, *Femininity in Flight*, 49.

32. Barry, *Femininity in Flight*, 47.

33. Pan American World Airways, "Win Your Wings as a Pan Am Stewardess," brochure, 1967, University of Miami Library, Special Collections, https://merrick.library.miami.edu/cdm/compoundobject/collection/asm0341/id/5616/rec/2.

34. Barry, *Femininity in Flight*, 114.

35. Barry, *Femininity in Flight*, 119.

36. Barry, *Femininity in Flight*, 120.

37. Sally Ride, "Sally Ride on Dumb Questions," interview by Gloria Steinem, Blank on Blank, June 18, 1983, https://blankonblank.org/interviews/sally-ride-space-shuttle-first-woman-space-nasa.

38. Sally Ride, "NASA Johnson Space Center Oral History Project Edited Oral History Transcript," interview by Rebecca Wright, National Aeronautics And Space Administration, October 22, 2002, https://historycollection.jsc.nasa.gov/JSCHistoryPortal/history/oral_histories/RideSK/RideSK_10-22-02.htm.

39. Rhea Seddon, "Diapers, Underwear, and Makeup," Rhea Seddon website, http://astronautrheaseddon.com/diapers-underwear-makeup, accessed March 1, 2020.

40. Robert Draper, "How Hillary Became 'Hillary,'" *New York Times*, October 11, 2016, https://www.nytimes.com/2016/10/16/magazine/how-hillary-clinton-became-hillary.html.

41. Claire Carusillo, "Meet the Makeup Artist Who Remade Hillary, Picked Lint off Bernie," Racked, March 21, 2016, https://www.racked.com/2016/3/21/11265376/makeup-artist-debate-kriss-soterin-blevens-ambers-place-heroin.

42. Eric Hehman et al., "Early Processing of Gendered Facial Cues Predicts the Electoral Success of Female Politicians," *Social Psychological and Personality Science* 5, no. 7 (2014): 815–24, https://doi.org/10.1177/1948550614534701.

43. Alexandria Ocasio-Cortez (@AOC), "Lip+hoops were inspired by Sonia Sotomayor . . ." Twitter, January 4, 2019, 2:21 p.m., https://twitter.com/AOC/status/1081284603850174467.

44. Shani Saxon-Parrish, "Her Honor: A Portrait of Justice Sonia Sotomayor," *Latina*, November 11, 2009, http://www.latina.com/lifestyle/news-politics/her-honor-portrait-justice-sonia-sotomayor.

45. Marilyn La Jeunesse, "21 Latinx People Get Real About What Red Lipstick Means to Them," *Teen Vogue*, October 2, 2018, https://www.teenvogue.com/story/latinx-people-on-red-lipstick.

46. Frances Solá-Santiago, "What Alexandria Ocasio-Cortez's Hoop Earrings Mean to Latina Women Like Me," *Glamour*, January 11, 2019, https://www.glamour.com/story/alexandria-ocasio-cortez-hoop-earrings.

47. Erynn Masi de Casanova, "Beauty Ideology in Latin America," *dObra[s]* 11, no. 23 (May 2018): 12–21, https://doi.org/10.26563/dobras .v11i23.708.

48. Erynn Masi de Casanova, *Making Up the Difference: Women, Beauty, and Direct Selling in Ecuador* (Austin: University of Texas Press, 2011), 127, Kindle.

49. Casanova, *Making Up the Difference*, 125, Kindle.

50. Casanova, *Making Up the Difference*, 123, Kindle.

51. Nicole Constable, *Maid to Order in Hong Kong: Stories of Migrant Workers, Second Edition* (Ithaca, NY: Cornell University Press, 2007), 3–4.

52. Constable, *Maid to Order in Hong Kong*, 74.

53. Constable, *Maid to Order in Hong Kong*, 175.

HEY, SEXY

1. Caity Weaver, "What Is Glitter?," *New York Times*, December 21, 2018, https://www.nytimes.com/2018/12/21/style/glitter-factory.html.

2. Elizabeth R. Escobedo, *From Coveralls to Zoot Suits: The Lives of Mexican American Women on the World War II Home Front* (Chapel Hill: University of North Carolina Press, 2013), 21, Kindle.

3. Arthur Miller, "Marilyn Monroe in a Remarkable Re-creation of Fabled Enchantresses," *Life*, December 22, 1958, 137, https://books.google .com/books?id=Yj8EAAAAMBAJ&printsec=frontcover&dq=marilyn +monroe&hl=en&sa=X&ved=2ahUKEwimroOgnqLrAhXKWc0KHWP eDQwQ6AEwB3oECAgQAg#v=onepage&q=marilyn%20monroe&f =false.

4. Madeleine Marsh, *Compacts and Cosmetics: Beauty from Victorian Times to the Present Day* (South Yorkshire, UK: Pen & Sword Books, 2009), loc. 1541–52, Kindle.

5. Marilyn E. Hegarty, *Victory Girls, Khaki-Wackies, and Patriotutes: The Regulation of Female Sexuality During World War II* (New York: New York University Press, 2008), 129–30, Kindle.

6. Page Dougherty Delano, "Making Up for War: Sexuality and Citizenship in Wartime Culture," *Feminist Studies* 26, no. 1 (Spring 2000): 33–68, https://www.jstor.org/stable/3178592.

7. Hegarty, *Victory Girls, Khaki-Wackies, and Patriotutes*, 12, Kindle.

8. Hegarty, *Victory Girls, Khaki-Wackies, and Patriotutes*, 142, Kindle.

9. Hegarty, *Victory Girls, Khaki-Wackies, and Patriotutes*, 144, Kindle.

10. Allison Glazebrook, "Cosmetics and Sôphrosunê: Ischomachos' Wife in Xenophon's Oikonomikos," *Classical World* 102, no. 3 (Spring 2009): 223–48, https://www.jstor.org/stable/40599847.

11. Carlota Batres et al., "Evidence That Makeup Is a False Signal of Sociosexuality," *Personality and Individual Differences* 122 (2018): 148–54, http://doi.org/10.1016/j.paid.2017.10.023.

12. Kristina Rodulfo, "Would You Wear No Makeup on the First Date?," *Elle*, July 27, 2018, https://www.elle.com/beauty/makeup-skin -care/a22092166/no-makeup-first-date.

13. Maria Ochoa, *Queen for a Day: Transformistas, Beauty Queens, and the Performance of Femininity in Venezuela* (Durham, NC: Duke University Press, 2014), 6, Kindle.

14. Ochoa, *Queen for a Day*, 3, Kindle.

15. Ochoa, *Queen for a Day*, 3, Kindle.

16. Ochoa, *Queen for a Day*, 216, Kindle.

17. Matt Houlbrook, "'The Man with the Powder Puff' in Interwar London," *Historical Journal* 50, no. 1 (March 2007): 145–71, https://www .jstor.org/stable/4140169.

18. Houlbrook, "'The Man with the Powder Puff' in Interwar London."

19. Escobedo, *From Coveralls to Zoot Suits*, 36, Kindle.

20. Escobedo, *From Coveralls to Zoot Suits*, 36, Kindle.

21. Escobedo, *From Coveralls to Zoot Suits*, 19, Kindle.

22. Catherine S. Ramírez, "Crimes of Fashion: The Pachuca and Chicana Style Politics," *Meridians* 2, no. 2 (2002): 1–35, https://www.jstor.org /stable/40338497.

23. Escobedo, *From Coveralls to Zoot Suits*, 26, Kindle.

24. Escobedo, *From Coveralls to Zoot Suits*, 28, Kindle.

25. Escobedo, *From Coveralls to Zoot Suits*, 29, Kindle.

26. Escobedo, *From Coveralls to Zoot Suits*, 28, Kindle.

27. Escobedo, *From Coveralls to Zoot Suits*, 28–29, Kindle.

28. Escobedo, *From Coveralls to Zoot Suits*, 21, Kindle.

29. Stacy L. Smith, Marc Choueiti, and Katherine Pieper, *Inclusion or Invisibility: Comprehensive Annenberg Report on Diversity in Entertainment* (Los Angeles: Media, Diversity & Social Change Initiative, Annenberg School for Communication and Journalism, USC, February 2016), https:// annenberg.usc.edu/sites/default/files/2017/04/07/MDSCI_CARD _Report_FINAL_Exec_Summary.pdf.

30. La Jeunesse, "21 Latinx People Get Real About What Red Lipstick Means to Them."

31. Marquaysa Battle, "Fenty Beauty Had a Powerful Message for a Fan Whose Lips Are 'Too Big' to Wear Red," Revelist, December 6, 2017, revelist.com/makeup/fenty-red-lipstick-big-lips/10755.

32. Teryn Payne, "Having Big Lips Was a Choice for Kylie Jenner— But Not for Me," *Glamour*, July 10, 2018, https://www.glamour.com/story /kylie-jenner-big-lips-injections.

33. Katherine Rosman, "The Model Whose Lips Spurred Racist Comments Speaks Out," *New York Times*, February 23, 2016, https://www .nytimes.com/2016/02/25/fashion/aamito-lagum-black-model-lips-mac -instagram.html.

34. Stunna Lip Pain Longwear Fluid Lip Color, https://www.fenty
beauty.com/stunna-lip-paint-longwear-fluid-lip-color/FB50002.html,
accessed December 28, 2020.

35. Fenty Beauty by Rihanna, "Tutorial Tuesdays with Rihanna:
#WILDTHOUGHTS," November 13, 2018, video, 5:55, https://www
.youtube.com/watch?v=YA0yaZiXFQU.

EXPANDING GENDER

1. Sally Pointer, *The Artifice of Beauty: A History and Practical Guide to
Perfume and Cosmetics* (Stroud, UK: Sutton, 2005), 19–20.

2. "Two Spirit," Indian Health Service, https://www.ihs.gov/lgbt
/health/twospirit/, accessed November 20, 2020.

3. Deborah A. Miranda, "Extermination of the Joyas: Gendercide in
Spanish California," *GLQ* 16, no. 1–2 (2010): 253–84, https://doi.org
/10.1215/10642684-2009-022.

4. Paul Douglas Campbell, *Earth Pigments and Paint of the California
Indians* (Los Angeles: Sunbelt, 2007), 60, 75–76, 143–146.

5. Miranda, "Extermination of the Joyas: Gendercide in Spanish
California."

6. Miranda, "Extermination of the Joyas: Gendercide in Spanish
California."

7. Miranda, "Extermination of the Joyas: Gendercide in Spanish
California."

8. Cherokee Nation, "Cherokee & Southeast Indian Tattooing," April 20,
2017, video, 24:00, https://www.youtube.com/watch?v=LV3KBgZDDO0.

9. William Bartram, *Travels and Other Writings* (1791; New York: Literary Classics of the United States, 1996), 291.

10. Peiss, *Hope in a Jar*, 23.

11. Geoffrey Jones, *Beauty Imagined: A History of the Global Beauty
Industry* (Oxford: Oxford University Press, 2010) 24, Kindle.

12. Jones, *Beauty Imagined*, 57, Kindle.

13. Meredith Talusan, "On Being a Trans Woman, and Giving Up
Makeup," *New York Times*, May 26, 2020, https://www.nytimes.com/2020
/05/26/opinion/trans-femininity.html.

14. Talusan, "On Being a Trans Woman, and Giving Up Makeup."

15. "Male Makeup: Going Mainstream in Asia and Slowly Gaining
Traction in the US," Coresight Research, April 24, 2019, https://coresight
.com/research/male-makeup-going-mainstream-in-asia-and-slowly
-gaining-traction-in-the-us.

16. David Yi, "For Korean Men, Groomed Eyebrows Is a Signifier of
Masculinity," Very Good Light, January 8, 2018, https://verygoodlight
.com/2018/01/08/for-korean-men-groomed-eyebrows-are-a-signifier
-of-masculinity/.

17. Kam Louie, "Popular Culture and Masculinity Ideals in East Asia, with Special Reference to China," *Journal of Asian Studies* 71, no. 4 (November 2012): 929–43, http://www.jstor.com/stable/23357427.

18. Louie, "Popular Culture and Masculinity Ideals in East Asia, with Special Reference to China."

19. Louie, "Popular Culture and Masculinity Ideals in East Asia, with Special Reference to China."

20. Morgan Neill, "Japan's 'Herbivore Men'—Less Interested in Sex, Money," CNN.com, June 8, 2009, http://edition.cnn.com/2009/WORLD /asiapcf/06/05/japan.herbivore.men/index.html.

21. Tomato Otake, "Blurring the Boundaries," *Japan Times*, May 10, 2009, https://www.japantimes.co.jp/life/2009/05/10/life/blurring-the -boundaries/#.Xup2VWpKiYV.

22. Yuen Shu Min, "Kusanagi Tsuyoshi x Chonangang: Transcending Japanese/Korean Ethnic Boundaries in Japanese Popular Culture," *Asian Studies Review* 35, no. 1 (March 2011): 1–20, http://dx.doi.org/10.1080 /10357823.2011.552708.

23. Neill, "Japan's 'Herbivore Men'—Less Interested in Sex, Money."

24. Maisie Skidmore, "Flash of Genius: Photographing Aladdin Sane," *AnOther*, December 23, 2015, https://www.anothermag.com/art -photography/8162/flash-of-genius-photographing-aladdin-sane.

25. Skidmore, "Flash of Genius: Photographing Aladdin Sane."

26. Peri Bradley and James Page, "David Bowie—The Trans Who Fell to Earth: Cultural Regulation, Bowie and Gender Fluidity," *Continuum* 31, no. 4 (2017): 583–95, https://doi.org/10.1080/10304312.2017.1334389.

27. James Charles (@jamescharles), "So I retook my senior photos & brought my ring light with me so my highlight would be poppin. I love being extra," Twitter, September 5, 2016, https://twitter.com/jamescharles /status/772883439733338112?ref_src=twsrc%5Etfw.

28. Valeria Safranova, "Meet CoverGirl's New Cover Boy," *New York Times*, October 12, 2016, https://www.nytimes.com/2016/10/16/fashion /meet-covergirls-new-cover-boy.html.

29. James Charles, YouTube Channel, as of July 1, 2020, https://www .youtube.com/channel/UCucot-Zp428OwkyRm2I7v2Q.

30. Safranova, "Meet CoverGirl's New Cover Boy."

31. David Yi, "Here's Where the Men's Beauty Industry Is Heading in 2020—And Beyond," Very Good Light, January 8, 2020, https://www .verygoodlight.com/2020/01/08/mens-beauty-2020.

32. Bella Cacciatore, "Brands Are Obsessed with Boys and Beauty. Is This a Passing Trend?," Very Good Light, August 29, 2017, https://www .verygoodlight.com/2017/08/29/boy-beauty.

33. Devon Abelman, "Khai Shares How Their Ever-Changing Makeup Represents Their Gender-Fluidity," *Allure*, June 15, 2020, https://www

.allure.com/story/blackbird-khai-butterfly-gender-fluidity-makeup-pride
-in-place.

34. Abelman, "Khai Shares How Their Ever-Changing Makeup Represents Their Gender-Fluidity."

35. Khai (@blackbirdkhai), "Lightning Fairy, raining down chaos pon your parade I used @bbo.beauty pigment powder & @suvabeauty Dance Party for this look," Instagram photo, March 11, 2020, https://www.instagram.com/p/B9nYvhQA9MG.

36. Khai (@blackbirdkhai), "Me trying to escape from reality," Instagram photo, November 18, 2019, https://www.instagram.com/p/B5B pouygoxw.

37. Khai (@blackbirdkhai), "Ouroboros: symbolizing the infinite cycle of life and how it sustains itself with (life)," Instagram photo, August 9, 2019, https://www.instagram.com/p/B09P9JdgWdI.

38. Abelman, "Khai Shares How Their Ever-Changing Makeup Represents Their Gender-Fluidity."

39. Matt Lubchansky, "Wearing Lipstick Was the Scariest Part of Saying Good-bye to My Male Identity," The Cut, October 10, 2018, https://www.thecut.com/2018/10/wearing-lipstick-helped-me-say-good-bye-to-my-male-identity.html.

SAFETY NOT GUARANTEED

1. Janet Mock, *Redefining Realness: My Path to Womanhood, Identity, Love & So Much More* (New York: Atria Paperback, 2014), 98.

2. Mock, *Redefining Realness*, 156.

3. Maxine E. Petersen and Robert Dickey, "Surgical Sex Reassignment: A Comparative Survey of International Centers," *Archives of Sexual Behavior* 24, no. 2 (1995): 135–56, https://doi.org/10.1007/BF01541578.

4. Lux Alptraum, "Makeup Can Give Trans Women Freedom—But It Can Also Take It Away," Racked, March 23, 2017, https://www.racked.com/2017/3/23/14937266/trans-women-makeup.

5. Mock, *Redefining Realness*, 112.

6. Tom Fitzgerald and Lorenzo Marquez, *Legendary Children: The First Decade of RuPaul's Drag Race and the Last Century of Queer Life* (New York: Penguin Books, 2020), 129.

7. *Paris Is Burning*, directed by Jennie Livingston (1990: Lionsgate, 18:00, Netflix).

8. Mock, *Redefining Realness*, 154.

9. *Paris Is Burning*, Livingston, 21:00.

10. Lukas Berredo et al., "Global Trans Perspectives on Health and Wellbeing: TvT Community Report," *Transrespect versus Transphobia Worldwide Project*, TvT Publication Series vol. 20 (December 2018), https://transrespect.org/wp-content/uploads/2018/12/TvT-PS-Vol20-2018_EN.pdf.

11. Mock, *Redefining Realness*, 177.

12. Janet Mock, "Being Pretty Is a Privilege, But We Refuse to Acknowledge It," *Allure*, June 28, 2017, https://www.allure.com/story/pretty-privilege.

13. Augusta Falletta and Meredith Talusan, "19 Insanely Useful Makeup Tips for Trans Women," BuzzFeed, April 12, 2016, https://www.buzzfeed.com/augustafalletta/makeup-tips-for-trans-women.

14. *Paris Is Burning*, Livingston, 54:02.

15. *Paris Is Burning*, Livingston, 1:09:08.

16. Rae Nudson, "In the 1920s, a Makeover Saved This Woman from the Death Penalty," Racked, January 26, 2018, https://www.racked.com/2018/1/26/16927682/makeover-death-penalty-sabella-nitti.

17. Genevieve Forbes, "Death for 2 Women Slayers," *Chicago Daily Tribune*, July 10, 1923, http://chicagotribune.newspapers.com/image/354955015, https://chicagotribune.newspapers.com/image/354955021, and http://chicagotribune.newspapers.com/image/354955235.

18. Nudson, "In the 1920s, a Makeover Saved This Woman from the Death Penalty."

19. Forbes, "Death for 2 Women Slayers."

20. Douglas Perry, *The Girls of Murder City: Fame, Lust, and the Beautiful Killers Who Inspired Chicago* (New York: Viking, 2010), 125.

21. Nudson, "In the 1920s, a Makeover Saved This Woman from the Death Penalty."

22. Perry, *The Girls of Murder City*, 122.

23. Perry, *The Girls of Murder City*, 45.

24. Perry, *The Girls of Murder City*, 72.

25. Genevieve Forbes, "Jail Can Really Do a Lot for a Woman," *Chicago Daily Tribune*, July 3, 1927, http://chicagotribune.newspapers.com/image/354914244.

26. Perry, *The Girls of Murder City*, 121.

27. Amanda Konradi, "Preparing to Testify: Rape Survivors Negotiating the Criminal Justice Process," *Gender and Society* 10, no. 4 (August 1996): 404–32, https://www.jstor.org/stable/189679.

28. Konradi, "Preparing to Testify: Rape Survivors Negotiating the Criminal Justice Process."

29. Caroline F. Keating et al., "Do Babyfaced Adults Receive More Help? The (Cross-Cultural) Case of the Lost Resume," *Journal of Nonverbal Behavior* 27, no. 2 (Summer 2003), https://www.ffri.hr/~ibrdar/komunikacija/seminari/Keating,%202003%20-%20Do%20babyfaced%20adults%20receive%20more%20help.pdf.

30. Alison Phipps, "Rape and Respectability: Ideas about Sexual Violence and Social Class," *Sociology* 43, no. 4 (August 2009): 667–83, https://www.jstor.org/stable/42857298.

31. Phipps, "Rape and Respectability: Ideas about Sexual Violence and Social Class."

32. Phipps, "Rape and Respectability: Ideas about Sexual Violence and Social Class."

33. "Irish Outcry over Teenager's Underwear Used in Rape Trial," BBC News, November 14, 2018, bbc.com/news/world-europe-46207304.

34. Clare Mulley, *The Spy Who Loved: The Secrets and Lives of Christine Granville* (New York: St. Martin's Press, 2012), 54–55, Kindle.

35. Ean Wood, *The Josephine Baker Story* (London: Omnibus Press, 2010), loc. 1893, Kindle.

36. "Josephine Baker, 1928–1930," Keystone-France/Gamma-Keystone via Getty Images, January 1, 1928, https://www.gettyimages.com/detail /news-photo/josephine-baker-1928-1930-news-photo/106507095.

37. Wood, *The Josephine Baker Story*, loc. 1951, Kindle.

38. Wood, *The Josephine Baker Story*, loc. 3978, Kindle.

39. Wood, *The Josephine Baker Story*, loc. 3274, Kindle.

40. Wood, *The Josephine Baker Story*, loc. 4079, Kindle.

41. Wood, *The Josephine Baker Story*, loc. 4276–4287, Kindle.

42. Wood, *The Josephine Baker Story*, loc. 4297, Kindle.

43. Wood, *The Josephine Baker Story*, loc. 4308, Kindle.

TOO FEW SHADES

1. A'Lelia Bundles, *On Her Own Ground: The Life and Times of Madam C. J. Walker* (New York: Washington Square Press, 2001), 62.

2. Bundles, *On Her Own Ground*, 60–61.

3. Marlen Komar, "Department Stores Are Basically the Reason Women Were Allowed in Public," Racked, February 8, 2018, https://www .racked.com/2018/2/9/16951116/department-stores-women-independence.

4. Peiss, *Hope in a Jar*, 221.

5. Bundles, *On Her Own Ground*, 276.

6. Bundles, *On Her Own Ground*, 200.

7. Bundles, *On Her Own Ground*, 248–49.

8. Henry Louis Gates Jr., "Who Was the 1st Black Millionairess?," The Root, June 24, 2013, https://www.theroot.com/who-was-the-1st-black -millionairess-1790897002.

9. Bundles, *On Her Own Ground*, 96.

10. Peiss, *Hope in a Jar*, 172.

11. Bundles, *On Her Own Ground*, 67.

12. Catherine Davenport, *Skin Deep: African American Women and the Building of Beauty Culture in South Carolina* (master's thesis, University of South Carolina, 2017), retrieved from https://scholarcommons.sc.edu /etd/4201.

13. Bundles, *On Her Own Ground*, 122.

14. National Museum of African American History & Culture, "Tin for Madam C. J. Walker's 'Tan-Off,'" accessed January 24, 2019, https://nmaahc.si.edu/object/nmaahc_2011.177.2.

15. Peiss, *Hope in a Jar*, 223.

16. Peiss, *Hope in a Jar*, 223.

17. Nadra Nittle, "Before Fenty: Over 100 Years of Black Makeup Brands," Racked, January 23, 2018, https://www.racked.com/2018/1/23/16901594/black-makeup-brands-history.

18. William J. Mahar, *Behind the Burnt Cork Mask: Early Blackface Minstrelsy and Antebellum American Popular Culture* (Urbana: University of Illinois Press, 1999), 1.

19. Mahar, *Behind the Burnt Cork Mask*, 28.

20. Karina Longworth, "147: Hattie McDaniel (Six Degrees of Song of the South, Episode 2)," October 29, 2019, in *You Must Remember This*, produced by Karina Longworth, podcast, 6:00, http://www.youmustrememberthispodcast.com/episodes/2019/10/23/hattie-mcdaniel-six-degrees-of-song-of-the-south-episode-2.

21. Donald Bogle, *Bright Boulevards, Bold Dreams: The Story of Black Hollywood* (New York: One World Books, 2005), 221.

22. Bogle, *Bright Boulevards, Bold Dreams*, 218.

23. Fred E. Basten, *Max Factor: The Man Who Changed the Faces of the World* (New York: Arcade, 2008), 138–39.

24. Bogle, *Bright Boulevards, Bold Dreams*, 219.

25. Bogle, *Bright Boulevards, Bold Dreams*, 219.

26. Karina Longworth, "33: Star Wars Episode VII: Lena Horne," February 17, 2015, in *You Must Remember This*, produced by Karina Longworth, podcast, 54:00, http://www.youmustrememberthispodcast.com/episodes/youmustrememberthispodcastblog/2015/2/17/star-wars-episode-vii-lena-horne.

27. Peiss, *Hope in a Jar*, 41.

28. Peiss, *Hope in a Jar*, 263.

29. Peiss, *Hope in a Jar*, 263.

30. Rachel Nussbaum, "CoverGirl's New TruBlend Matte Made Foundation Comes in 40 Shades, *Glamour*, May 7, 2018, https://www.glamour.com/story/covergirl-trublend-matte-made-foundation-40-shades.

31. Layla Ilchi, "Fenty Beauty Earns Third Spot in Earned Media Value," *WWD*, October 24, 2017, https://wwd.com/beauty-industry-news/color-cosmetics/fenty-beauty-earns-third-spot-earned-media-value-after-launch-11034624.

32. Grand View Research, "Skin Lightening Products Market Size, Share & Trends Analysis Report by Product (Cream, Cleanser, Mask), by Nature (Synthetic, Natural, Organic), by Region, and Segment Forecasts, 2019–2025," August 2019, https://www.grandviewresearch.com/industry-analysis/skin-lightening-products-market; Grand View Research, "Skin

Lightening Products Market Size Worth $13.7 Billion by 2025," August 2019, https://www.grandviewresearch.com/press-release/global-skin -lightening-products-market.

33. Rebekah Kebede, "Why Black Women in a Predominately Black Culture Are Still Bleaching Their Skin," *Marie Claire*, June 21, 2017, https://www.marieclaire.com/beauty/a27678/skin-bleaching-epidemic -in-jamaica.

34. Tara John and Swati Gupta, "Photograph of Miss India Finalists Stirs Debate over Country's Obsession with Fair Skin," CNN.com, May 31, 2019, https://www.cnn.com/style/article/miss-india-fairness-intl /index.html.

35. Tan France with Caroline Donofrio, *Naturally Tan* (New York: St. Martin's Press, 2019), 234–5.

36. Davenport, *Skin Deep*.

37. Coco Khan, "Skin-Lightening Creams Are Dangerous—Yet Business Is Booming. Can the Trade Be Stopped?," *The Guardian*, April 23, 2018, https://www.theguardian.com/world/2018/apr/23/skin-lightening -creams-are-dangerous-yet-business-is-booming-can-the-trade-be-stopped.

38. Andrea Arterberry, "Why Are Women of Color Still Having Trouble Finding Foundation?," *Cosmopolitan*, December 26, 2015, https:// www.cosmopolitan.com/style-beauty/beauty/news/a50647/women-of-color -makeup-foundation.

39. Tansy Breshears, "The Insidious Racism of Drugstore Beauty," Racked, September 28, 2017, https://www.racked.com/2017/9/28/16368722 /makeup-racism-fenty-beauty.

POW(D)ERFUL

1. Jonathan Clements, *Wu: The Chinese Empress Who Schemed, Seduced and Murdered Her Way to Become a Living God* (Stroud, UK: Sutton, 2007), 238.

2. Rebecca Doran, *Transgressive Typologies: Constructions of Gender and Power in Early Tang China* (Cambridge, MA: Harvard University Press, 2016), 2.

3. N. Harry Rothschild, *Wu Zhao: China's Only Woman Emperor* (New York: Pearson Longman, 2008), 13.

4. Charles Benn, *China's Golden Age: Everyday Life in the Tang Dynasty* (Oxford, UK: Oxford University Press, 2002), 108.

5. Benn, *China's Golden Age*, 108.

6. Clements, *Wu*, 168.

7. Rothschild, *Wu Zhao*, 101.

8. Rothschild, *Wu Zhao*, 203.

9. Clements, *Wu*, 45.

10. Rothschild, *Wu Zhao*, 29–30.

11. Clements, *Wu*, 67.

12. Clements, *Wu*, 74.

13. Benn, *China's Golden Age*, 108.

14. Benn, *China's Golden*, 110.

15. BuYun Chen, *Empire of Style: Silk and Fashion in Tang China* (Seattle: University of Washington Press, 2019), 53.

16. N. Harry Rothschild, author and professor of Asian history at the University of North Florida, in discussion with the author, December 6, 2019.

17. Rothschild, *Wu Zhao*, 203.

18. Alison Weir, *The Life of Elizabeth I* (New York: Ballantine Books, 1998), 238–39, Kindle.

19. Weir, *The Life of Elizabeth I*, 239, Kindle.

20. Lisa Eldridge, *Face Paint: The Story of Makeup* (New York: Abrams Image, 2015), 50.

21. Weir, *The Life of Elizabeth I*, 235–36, Kindle.

22. Eleanor Herman, *The Royal Art of Poison: Filthy Palaces, Fatal Cosmetics, Deadly Medicine, and Murder Most Foul* (New York: St. Martin's Press, 2018), 32.

23. Herman, *The Royal Art of Poison*, 38.

24. Sarah E. Schaffer, "Reading Our Lips: The History of Lipstick Regulation in Western Seats of Power," *Food and Drug Law Journal* 62, no. 1 (2007) 165–225, https://www.jstor.org/stable/26660916.

25. Rebecca Onion, "The Real Story Behind Margot Robbie's Wild Queen Elizabeth Makeup," Slate, December 6, 2018, https://slate.com /technology/2018/12/queen-elizabeth-makeup-margot-robbie-mary -queen-of-scots-real-story.html.

26. Miranda Kaufmann, *Black Tudors: The Untold Story* (London: Oneworld Publications, 2017), 1–2.

27. Yumna Siddiqi, "Dark Incontinents: The Discourses of Race and Gender in Three Renaissance Masques," *Renaissance Drama* 23 (1992): 141, https://www.jstor.org/stable/41917287.

28. Robert Hume, "Reflecting on Beauty: Maria Gunning's Sad Story," *Irish Examiner*, July 25, 2018, https://www.irishexaminer.com/lifestyle /arid-30857470.html.

29. Arabelle Sicardi, "I Attended a 50-Step Contouring Class with Kim Kardashian West," Racked, August 10, 2015, https://www.racked.com/2015 /8/10/9117195/kim-kardashian-mario-dedivanovic-contouring-secrets.

30. Lindsay Peoples, "An Open Letter to My White Friends Who Love the Kardashians," The Cut, July 20, 2015, https://www.thecut.com/2015/07 /my-white-friends-who-love-the-kardashians.html.

THE COST OF BEAUTY

1. Woodhead, *War Paint*, 25.

2. Woodhead, *War Paint*, 62.

3. Woodhead, *War Paint*, 62.

4. Basten, *Max Factor*, 52.

5. Woodhead, *War Paint*, 238.

6. Woodhead, *War Paint*, 72.

7. Woodhead, *War Paint*, 221.

8. Woodhead, *War Paint*, 102–3; photo courtesy of the Elizabeth Arden Archives, New York.

9. Woodhead, *War Paint*, 220–21; photo courtesy of the Elizabeth Arden Archives, New York.

10. Woodhead, *War Paint*, 185.

11. Tiffany M. Gill, *Beauty Shop Politics: African American Women's Activism in the Beauty Industry* (Urbana: University of Illinois Press, 2010), 19, Kindle.

12. Evelyn Northington, "Good Spirits Make Good Looks," *Half Century Magazine* 1, no. 1 (August 1916): 11–14, https://babel.hathitrust.org /cgi/pt?id=uiug.30112002019278&view=1up&seq=11.

13. Gill, *Beauty Shop Politics*, 51, Kindle.

14. Gill, *Beauty Shop Politics*, 52, Kindle.

15. Gill, *Beauty Shop Politics*, 107, Kindle.

16. Gill, *Beauty Shop Politics*, 107, Kindle.

17. Gill, *Beauty Shop Politics*, 65, Kindle.

18. Gill, *Beauty Shop Politics*, 65, Kindle.

19. Gill, *Beauty Shop Politics*, 104, Kindle.

20. Peiss, *Hope in a Jar*, 245–46.

21. Katina L. Manko, "'Now You Are in Business for Yourself': The Independent Contractors of the California Perfume Company, 1886–1938," *Business and Economic History* 26, no. 1 (Fall 1997): 5–26, http://www.jstor .com/stable/23703297.

22. Manko, "'Now You Are in Business for Yourself.'"

23. Manko, "'Now You Are in Business for Yourself.'"

24. Kathy Peiss, "On Beauty . . . and the History of Business."

25. Jane Marie, "Women's Work," September 24, 2018, in *The Dream*, produced by Laura Mayer, Chris Bannon, Dann Gallucci, and Jane Marie, podcast, 13:58, https://www.stitcher.com/podcast/stitcher/the-dream/e /56394468.

26. Gao Chong, "Embeddedness and Virtual Community: Chinese Women and Online Shopping," in *Chinese Women and the Cyberspace*, ed. Khun Eng Kuah-Pearce (Amsterdam: Amsterdam University Press, 2008), 135–53, http://www.jstor.com/stable/j.ctt46mvqc.11.

27. Gao, "Embeddedness and Virtual Community Chinese Women and Online Shopping."

28. Gao, "Embeddedness and Virtual Community Chinese Women and Online Shopping."

29. Gao, "Embeddedness and Virtual Community Chinese Women and Online Shopping."

30. Tati, "Free Stuff Beauty Gurus Get | Unboxing PR Packages . . . Episode 17," January 11, 2019, video, 22:13, https://www.youtube.com/watch?v=wgIKs4SwlgY.

31. Claire Carusillo, "Infiltrating Makeup Alley, the Internet's Most Secretive Community of Beauty Obsessives," Racked, August 5, 2015, https://www.racked.com/2015/8/5/9095857/makeup-alley-beauty-reviews-message-boards.

32. M. Shahbandeh, "Growth Rate of the Global Cosmetics Market 2004–2019," Statista, March 18, 2020, https://www.statista.com/statistics/297070/growth-rate-of-the-global-cosmetics-market.

33. M. Shahbandeh, "Cosmetics Industry—Statistics & Facts," Statista, January 22, 2020, https://www.statista.com/topics/3137/cosmetics-industry/#:~:text=Skincare%20was%20the%20leading%20category,for%202019%20percent%20in%202018.

34. Julie Creswell, "Why Get All Made Up With Nowhere to Go?," New York Times, May 8, 2020, https://www.nytimes.com/2020/05/08/business/coronavirus-makeup-hair-skin-care.html?campaign_id=2&emc=edit_th_200512&instance_id=18406&nl=todaysheadlines&regi_id=48128556&segment_id=27357&user_id=64b68a284d9e1bcce4d583734e6bdab4.

35. Lauren Cochrane, "Is There a Dark Side to the Growing Obsession with Skincare?," Guardian, June 21, 2018, https://www.theguardian.com/fashion/2018/jun/21/is-there-dark-side-to-growing-obsession-with-skincare.

36. Krithika Varagur, "The Skincare Con," The Outline, January 30, 2018, https://theoutline.com/post/3151/the-skincare-con-glossier-drunk-elephant-biologique-recherche-p50?zd=2&zi=fpmy72y4.

37. Peiss, "On Beauty . . . and the History of Business."

TOOLS OF RESISTANCE

1. The Laws of New York Consolidated Laws, Penal, Loitering § 240.35, https://www.nysenate.gov/legislation/laws/PEN/240.35.

2. George Chauncey, Gay New York: Gender, Urban Culture, and the Making of the Gay Male World, 1890–1940 (New York: BasicBooks, 1994), 343, Kindle.

3. David Carter, Stonewall: The Riots That Sparked the Gay Revolution (New York: St. Martin's Griffin, 2004), 15.

4. Chauncey, Gay New York, 194–95, Kindle.

5. Chauncey, Gay New York, 195, Kindle.

6. Desmond Vincent, "I Risk My Life to Wear Nail Polish. This Is Why I Still Do It," Very Good Light, January 16, 2020, https://verygoodlight.com/2020/01/16/nail-nigeria.

7. Carter, Stonewall, 69.

8. Carter, Stonewall, 77.

9. Carter, *Stonewall*, 132.

10. Tourmaline, "Sylvia Rivera & NYPD Reflect on Stonewall Rebellion," The Spirit Was . . . , February 22, 2012, https://thespiritwas.tumblr.com/post/18108920192/sylvia-rivera-nypd-reflect-on-stonewall.

11. Carter, *Stonewall*, 148.

12. Carter, *Stonewall*, 130.

13. Eric Marcus, "Sylvia Rivera—Part 2," October 21, 2017, in *Making Gay History*, produced by Sara Burningham, podcast, https://makinggayhistory.com/podcast/sylvia-rivera-part-2.

14. Tourmaline, "Marsha P. Johnson Photo by Randy Wicker," The Spirit Was . . . , March 13, 2012, https://thespiritwas.tumblr.com/post/19250274097/marsha-p-johnson-photo-by-randy-wicker.

15. Fitzgerald and Marquez, *Legendary Children*, 16.

16. Eric Marcus, "Marsha P. Johnson & Randy Wicker," March 1, 2017, in *Making Gay History*, produced by Sara Burningham, podcast, https://makinggayhistory.com/podcast/episode-11-johnson-wicker.

17. Marcus, "Marsha P. Johnson & Randy Wicker."

18. Marcus, "Marsha P. Johnson & Randy Wicker."

19. Sylvia Rivera, "L020A Sylvia Rivera, 'Y'all Better Quiet Down' Original Authorized Video by LoveTapesCollective, 1973 Gay Pride Rally NYC," LoveTapesCollective, June 24, 1973, video, https://vimeo.com/234353103.

20. Jessie Yeung, "Some Hong Kong Protesters Are Adopting the Joker as Their Own. Others Are Horrified," CNN.com, October 29, 2019, https://www.cnn.com/2019/10/29/asia/hong-kong-protests-joker-intl-hnk-scli/index.html.

21. Stella Ko, "'Beauty Is Freedom': The North Korean Millennials Wearing Makeup to Rebel Against the State," CNN.com, March 3, 2020, https://www.cnn.com/style/article/north-korea-womens-beauty-freedom/index.html.

22. Ko, "'Beauty Is Freedom': The North Korean Millennials Wearing Makeup to Rebel Against the State."

23. Juliet Perry, "North Korea Tourist Photos, as Seen by Defectors," CNN.com, December 15, 2016, https://www.cnn.com/travel/article/north-korea-nk-news-defectors/index.html.

24. Houchang E. Chehabi, "Staging the Emperor's New Clothes: Dress Codes and Nation-Building Under Reza Shah," *Iranian Studies* 26, nos. 3–4 (1993): 209–33, https://doi.org/10.1080/00210869308701800.

25. Patricia Marx, "About Face," *New Yorker*, March 16, 2015, https://www.newyorker.com/magazine/2015/03/23/about-face.

26. Alexandra Stevenson, "South Korea Loves Plastic Surgery and Makeup. Some Women Want to Change That," *New York Times*, November 23, 2018, https://www.nytimes.com/2018/11/23/business/south-korea-makeup-plastic-surgery-free-the-corset.html.

27. Marx, "About Face."

28. Stevenson, "South Korea Loves Plastic Surgery and Makeup. Some Women Want to Change That."

29. Stevenson, "South Korea Loves Plastic Surgery and Makeup. Some Women Want to Change That."

30. Evette Dionne, *Lifting as We Climb: Black Women's Battle for the Ballot Box* (New York: Viking, 2020), 103, Kindle.

31. Charlotte Curtis, "Miss America Pageant Is Picketed by 100 Women," *New York Times*, September 8, 1968, https://www.nytimes.com/1968/09/08 /archives/miss-america-pageant-is-picketed-by-100-women.html.

32. Curtis, "Miss America Pageant Is Picketed by 100 Women."

33. Roxane Gay, "Fifty Years Ago, Protesters Took on the Miss America Pageant and Electrified the Feminist Movement," *Smithsonian Magazine*, January 2018, https://www.smithsonianmag.com/history/fifty -years-ago-protestors-took-on-miss-america-pageant-electrified-feminist -movement-180967504.

34. Constance Grady, "The Waves of Feminism, and Why People Keep Fighting over Them, Explained," Vox, July 20, 2018, https://www.vox.com /2018/3/20/16955588/feminism-waves-explained-first-second-third-fourth.

35. Cheryl Wischhover, "Talking to Chimamanda Ngozi Adichie, the Beauty Brand Ambassador We All Need Right Now," Racked, November 22, 2016, https://www.racked.com/2016/11/22/13714228/chimamanda -ngozi-adichie-boots-beauty.

36. Alicia Keys, "Alicia Keys: Time to Uncover," Lenny Letter, May 31, 2016, https://www.lennyletter.com/story/alicia-keys-time-to-uncover.

37. Penelope Green, "Alicia Keys and the 'Tyranny of Makeup,'" *New York Times*, September 14, 2016, https://www.nytimes.com/2016/09/15 /fashion/alicia-keys-no-makeup-beauty-movement.html.

38. Green, "Alicia Keys and the 'Tyranny of Makeup.'"

39. Amnesty International, "Nicaragua: Shoot to Kill: Nicaragua's Strategy to Repress Protest," Amnesty International, index no.: AMR 43/8470/2018, May 28, 2018, https://www.amnesty.org/en/documents /amr43/8470/2018/en.

40. Confidencial, "José Dolores Blandino y la Asociación de Mujeres del 'Pico Rojo,'" October 16, 2018, video, trans. Abigail Weinberg, https:// www.youtube.com/watch?v=1oh-upYg1K4&feature=youtu.be.

41. Confidencial, "José Dolores Blandino y la Asociación de Mujeres del 'Pico Rojo,'" video, 6:16.

42. Confidencial, "José Dolores Blandino y la Asociación de Mujeres del 'Pico Rojo,'" video, 6:16.

43. Confidencial, "José Dolores Blandino y la Asociación de Mujeres del 'Pico Rojo,'" video, 7:48.

44. Confidencial, "José Dolores Blandino y la Asociación de Mujeres del 'Pico Rojo,'" video, 7:48.

45. Confidencial, "José Dolores Blandino y la Asociación de Mujeres del 'Pico Rojo,'" video, 7:48.

46. Andalusia Knoll Soloff, "In Mexico, Women Are Protesting a Wave of Brutal Murders with Performance," Vice, March 25, 2016, https://www.vice.com/en_us/article/ezjejp/in-mexico-women-are-protesting-a-wave-of-brutal-murders-with-performance.

47. Soloff, "In Mexico, Women Are Protesting a Wave of Brutal Murders with Performance."

48. Jean-François Lozier, "A Nicer Red: The Exchange and Use of Vermilion in Early America," *Eighteenth-Century Studies* 51, no. 1 (Fall 2017): 45–61, https://doi.org/10.1353/ecs.2017.0046.

49. Ruth Hopkins, "The Use of War Paint in Native Communities Is Evolving," *Teen Vogue*, April 10, 2020, https://www.teenvogue.com/story/use-war-paint-native-communities.

PHOTO CREDITS

Page 1: (Clockwise from top) DeAgostini/Getty Images; National Portrait Gallery; British Library

Page 2: Smithsonian Institution, National Museum of American History (top); *Chicago Tribune* archives/TCA (bottom)

Page 3: The Hollywood Archive (top); Allstar Picture Library, Ltd./Alamy (middle); Keystone Press/ Alamy (bottom)

Page 4: Pictorial Press Ltd./Alamy (top); Associated Press (middle); Pan American World Airways, Inc. records (bottom)

Page 5: ilpo musto/Alamy (top); Randolfe Wicker (bottom)

Page 6: (Clockwise from top): Kyodo News; AFP/AFP via Getty Images; Image Press Agency/Alamy

Page 7: dpa picture alliance/Alamy (top); AP Photo/ J. Scott Applewhite (bottom)

Page 8: RJ Sangosti/MediaNews Group/*Denver Post* via Getty Images (top); Everett Collection Inc./Alamy

INDEX

Abdul-Mateen, Yahya, 109
Abtey, Jacques, 94–95
Adichie, Chimamanda Ngozi,
169–70
African American beauty products:
beauty tips for, 143; color tones,
113–14; "ethnic" cosmetics, 110;
High-Brown Face Powder, 105,
142; Light Egyptian, 108–9;
Patti's Beauty Emporium,
105; Tan-Off, 103–4; Valmor
Products, 105; Wonderful Face
Bleach, 103, 113. *See also* Fenty;
skin lightening and bleaching
products
African American women:
#ActingWhileBlack, 109–10;
#Nomakeup, 170–71; cosmet-
ics and hair products, 100–102;
dress code and makeup, 17;
film industry, 106–10; flight
attendants, 26–27; folk recipes
for skin care, 104; Kardashian
features, 132; lip size, 54; racism
and colorism, 97–99; respectability politics, 161; royal courts
and, 128; salons for, 142–44; segregation and department stores,
99; slavery and beauty standards,
98; slavery and sexuality, 53;

suffrage march treatment, 9,
168. *See also* Baker, Josephine;
Madam Walker, C. J.; Mock,
Janet; skin lightening and
bleaching
Aladdin Sane (Bowie), 70
Alegria, Claribel, 172
Allure, 74, 81
Alptraum, Lux, 78
Amador, Manuel, 173
Amnesty International, 171
Anderson, Otis, 42
Anglo-American society, 62–63;
expanded gender roles with
makeup, 69–70, 72; heavy
makeup in, 136–37; lady's maids
and, 137; upper-class women, 9,
11, 64, 129–30
appearance politics, 1, 11, 169
Arden, Elizabeth: Arden's Maine
Chance, 140; Marine Corps
makeup kit, 23; red lipsticks,
141; salons, 64, 138–39, 142;
white upper-class market,
104–5, 151
Arterbery, Andrea, 113
Asia-Pacific people: Boy de Chanel
in S. Korea, 73; herbivore men,
57–69; historical use of makeup,
69; male grooming products,